SIMPLE SOLUTIONS

A TRIP INTO SUSTAINABLE WELL-CARE

EKELE UKEGBU-NWANKWO, BCC, DNOM, D.MIN

Simple Solutions

A Trip Into Sustainable Well-Care

By Ekele P. Ukegbu-Nwankwo
BCC, DNOM, CHC, D. Min

SIMPLE SOLUTIONS:
A TRIP INTO SUSTAINABLE WELL-CARE

Copyright © 2019 by Ekele P. Ukegbu-Nwankwo
ISBN: 978-0-578-53237-0

All rights reserved. No part of this publication may be reproduced, stored, or transmitted in any form or by any means, electronic, mechanical, photocopying, recording, scanning, or otherwise, except as permitted under Section 107 or 108 of the 1976 United States Copyright Act, without the prior written permission of the author. Requests to the author and publisher for permission should be addressed to the following email: info@liv-n-glow.com

Limitation of liability/disclaimer of warranty. While the publisher and author have used their best efforts in providing helpful and useful content in this book, they make no representations or warranties with respect to the accuracy or completeness of the contents of this document and specifically disclaim any implied warranties of merchantability or fitness for particular purpose.

The advice and strategies contained therein may not be suitable for your situation. You should consult with a professional where appropriate. Neither the publisher nor author shall be liable for any loss of health, profit or any other commercial damages, including but not limited to special, incidental, consequential, or other damages.

Be advised, all scriptures are from the King James Version unless otherwise noted.

First Printing July 2019
Printed in the United States of America
Published by: Executive Business Writing
Edited by: JB Editing Solutions
Cover Design: LLC Media Productions, LLC

As the bird by wandering, as the swallow by flying, so the curse causeless shall not come. Proverb 26:2

Having therefore these promises, dearly beloved, let us cleanse ourselves from all filthiness of the flesh and spirit, perfecting holiness in the fear of God.
2 Corinthians 7:1

*Know ye that the L*ORD *He is God: it is He that hath made us, and not we ourselves; we are His people, and the sheep of His pasture.* Psalm 100:3

"The doctor of the future will give no medicine but will interest his patient in the care of the human frame, in diet and in the cause and prevention of disease."
Thomas Edison (1903)

Table of Contents

Dedication 1

Acknowledgements 3

Introduction 7

An Original Foundation 9
    Biblical Background to Healthful Living 11
    Historical Perspective of Food and Health 21
    Importance of Herbs/Greens 24
    Disease and Lifespan 28
    Evolution of Eating Patterns 34
    Vegetarian, Vegan, or Health Reformer 36
    Seventh-day Adventist Perspectives on Food and Nutrition 45
    Contribution of the "China Doctor" 50

Food and the Body 51
    Carbohydrates 57
    Fats 60
    Other Groups 61
    Needs of the Cell 62

Disease and Nutrition 66
    Disease Movement 67
    Disease and Culture 70
    Food Supplementation 76
    The Original Diet 78
    Death or Life in the Kitchen 80
    Change of Taste Buds 82
    Affluent Malnutrition and the Protein Myth 82
    So, What Should We Eat? 85
    The Doctor of the Kitchen 86
    Bean Cookery 89
    So, When Should We Eat? 93
    One Hundred Years Ahead of Her Time 98

Lifestyle and Holistic Living 102

- Eight Most Esteemed Doctors – God's Plan 102
- The Issue of Rest 109
- Uncommon Remedies for Common Illnesses 113
- Meatless Recipes 115
- Suggested Recovery Menu Guide 136
- Nutrient Hierarchy 139
- Images of Real Food 141
- SAD and GLAD Diets 142
- Fiber Foods 144
- Herbs and Healing 144
- Therapeutic Grade Essential Oils 150

General Guidelines for Multi-Cellular Living 164

- Guidelines for Optimal Health 166
- Two-Week Meal Challenge 177
- Summary and Conclusion 181
- Natural Remedies 183

Author's Biographical Sketch 206

- Contact Information 207

Appendix 208

- Some Tropical Fruits and Vegetables of Nigeria and West Africa 208

Notes 220

Table of Tables

Table 1. Contrast Between Vegans and Health Reformers 43
Table 2. Disease Groupings Observed in Rural China 83
Table 3. Sample Menu Suggestion for Three Meals Per Day ... 94
Table 4. I Was Shown's 98
Table 5. Eight Most Esteemed Doctors 102
Table 6. Suggested Recovery Menu Guide 136
Table 7. Additional Meal Combination Options 138
Table 8. SAD and GLAD Diets 142
Table 9. Fiber Foods 144
Table 10. Herbs, Spices, and Essential Oils 145
Table 11. Simple Two-Week Meal Plan 179

Table of Figures

Figure 1. Clean and unclean food 18
Figure 2. Grains, fruits, nuts, and vegetables 25
Figure 3. Egyptian mummy 27
Figure 4. Lifespans before and after Noah's flood 30
Figure 5. Ten generations before the flood 31
Figure 6. Ten generations after the flood 31
Figure 7. Dramatic size reduction 32
Figure 8. Illness-Wellness continuum 70
Figure 9. Hezekiah's healing 114
Figure 10. Vita-Flex foot chart 158
Figure 11. Eat from recommended categories of food 176

Dedication

To my oldest sister, Ukachi Ikpeoha, and my brothers – Dr. Okezie, Acho, Emeka, and Dr. Charles (Nonye) Ukegbu, without whom my family and I would not have made it to the USA, where I embraced this message of lifestyle change to the fullest. My other older sisters, Onyinye Nwosu and Nwozichi Onyekwere played significant roles, calling, cheering, and encouraging. I will always remember my sister, Nwanyi Obasi, whom we lost long before I commenced this project. Being in the field of nutrition and home economics, she would have been of immense help.

Acknowledgements

My younger sister, Enyioma Anaba, for sheltering me when I most needed a place of refuge, understanding my need for extra time at home to work on the book, quite often before coming to work in our shared office. She often asked how much more time I needed and was always ready to sacrifice extra time so I could leave early to continue my writing or prepare for a healthy living event.

My older brother, Dr. Okezie Ukegbu, a physician assistant and chiropractor, for sacrificing several hours to proofread and offer suggestions as the work progressed. Many of the Bible texts used at the beginning of the chapters are memory verses learned at a very young age from the daily early morning devotions led by our beloved parents.

Mrs. Shirley Iheanacho, my teacher during my first year of the Business Typing college course in the (then) Adventist College of West Africa (ACWA), Nigeria. Since we reconnected again after several years, Sister Shirley, as I call her, never ceased to inspire me from her own and several other peoples' experiences, to rise up and share with the world my personal struggles, my knowledge and passion in the work of health reform, and my ministry as a chaplain. She has been a great mentor in this journey.

Dr. Kwesi Gyimah, for informing me about the possibility of literature evangelistic work at a time when my world seemed to have tumbled beyond possible redemption. From the moment he learned I was writing a book, he often checked, cheering me to 'get it done.'

Larry Fleming, for his willingness to teach, correct, share, and inspire me to ensure that my bearings must always align with the principles laid down in the Bible and the inspired writings of Ellen G. White. As a seasoned cook for over forty years and an experienced international restaurant evangelist, brother Larry was always available, whether at home or abroad, to answer my questions on cooking/meal creation or health consultation with the sick. He was quick to refer me to new videos or research works that confirm our belief in plant-based living and the tenets of the health message.

Dr. Marian Atolagbe and Joy Chidinma Michael (my cousin), both of whom were my consultants anytime I needed extra counsel with the use of local herbs for persons in Nigeria; Ngozi Enemanna, RN, who continued to encourage and direct me further in the use of natural remedies and, sometimes, supplements which aided and sustained her husband for sixteen years of an invasive debilitating cancer, which eventually took his life.

Dr. Lidia Hicks, who introduced and mentored me in the use of natural essential oils and stood by me to ensure growth and expertise in their use for treatment of disease.

Stacey Kimbrell, a natural health and chemical awareness advocate, who authored the book, *Living Balanced*, has been a great mentor in the world of essential oils and chemical toxicity. Her book is always a great resource.

Elder Mamon Wilson and his wife (now passed), at whose feet I sat for thirty days, learning the implications of health reform, it's connection to the gospel, and the work of preparation for the second coming of Christ.

The Health Ministry Leadership of the North Eastern Conference (NEC) of New York, who gave me initial training and thus sparked my appetite in the medical missionary endeavor.

This work has been designed with the intention of helping the reader appreciate videos that capture particular lifestyle and medical practices that help or hinder wellness. Getting such videos into this book would not have been possible without the advanced and specialized computer skills of Ali A. Sheriff. Ali, who is a computer instructor, made himself available to assist and guide me even on his off days, Fridays, when he should have been praying in the mosque.

I am grateful to my children, Ihuoma, Ogechi, Enyioma and Chinagozi, whose continued support in various ways motivated me to write on the subject of healthful living. They have not only seen my passion but continue to experience the benefits of the application of the lifestyle in their daily living.

Introduction

This book is designed as a supplemental instruction to the health seeker. The reader will be able to glean special pieces of advice that will enable him/her to make informed decisions regarding healthful living and spiritual matters as well. The work of healing is like the work of the Holy Spirit. He woos the degenerate mind gradually to understand and live the principles of right doing and living. So also does the work of healing take some time to win the degenerated and compromised body system, organ, or tissue back to normalcy. As the **dis-ease** took its time to develop in the body, so also will the system take time to restore **ease** to the body. The sick person needs patient endurance. Cooperation with the divine healer who only brings about healing using remedial approaches that are compatible to His original design, is the ultimate requirement.

Chapter 1

An Original Foundation

It might be surprising for some persons to find that the subject of physical health and healing has foundations from God's word – the Bible, a sacred book that is known and referred to mostly for spiritual concerns of living. God has something better for man in that He is as concerned about the spiritual wellbeing as He is about the physical. This is because as the Creator, He knows that the state of health influences judgment, mind, willpower – all faculties that are pivotal to understanding and making intelligent decisions. We see throughout Scripture that God is concerned about our health. Many texts from both Old and New Testaments testify to this fact, as seen from just these few selections:

> 1 Corinthians 6:19,20: *What? know ye not that your body is the temple of the Holy Ghost, which is in you, which ye have of God, and ye are not your own? For ye are bought with a price: therefore, glorify God in your body, and in your spirit, which are God's.*
>
> Exodus 15:26: *If thou wilt diligently hearken to the voice of the Lord thy God, and wilt do that which is right in his sight, and wilt give ear to his commandments, and keep all his statutes, I will put none of these diseases upon thee, which I have brought upon the Egyptians: for I am the Lord that healeth thee.*

An Original Foundation

God also gave a reason for giving the instruction; He considers those who have chosen to believe in Him to be a holy people.

> Deuteronomy 14:2: *For thou art an holy people unto the LORD thy God, and the LORD hath chosen thee to be a peculiar people unto himself, above all the nations that are upon the earth.*

These imply that God loves order and decency and wants a clean and wholesome place to reside. When Jesus walked upon the earth, the wealthy did not value Him so He walked among the poor of the land and taught them the principles of life on earth and preparation for the heavenly life. Then He invited them to follow His example. These few lowly ranked followers preserved the Word and transformed the world. Christ's method is supported by a famous statement by the second United States President, John Adams who said in 1775,

> *"The preservation of the means of knowledge among the lowest ranks is of more importance to the public than all the property of all the rich men in the country."*

Yes, wealth and means come and vanish away, but the principles of the Word for daily living continue to circulate among all ranks and file of society until the end of time.

Biblical Background to Healthful Living

At creation God in His foreknowledge created man and gave him what was best for his biological needs (Genesis 1:29), which was basically plant-based nutrition. God says all He made 'was good' (Genesis 1:31). Everything God made is good for the purpose for which He made it. Further along the line, the flood came and wiped out vegetation. After the flood, God permitted the eating of flesh, specified animals that were to be eaten, as seen in Deuteronomy 14:3-21 and Leviticus 11:1-47. However, God earlier made that distinction when He instructed Noah to order the animals into the ark. He told Noah to take into the ark **two** pairs each of every unclean animal, male and female and **seven** pairs each of every clean one, male and female as well (Genesis 7:2-3). God made scavengers that fly in the air; those that swim in the oceans, seas, lakes, rivers, and streams; and those that walk on land.

God forbade for food any creatures that creep, except those insects that fly and have jointed legs (see Leviticus 11:21 and Deuteronomy 14:19). During the exodus, God warned the children of Israel not to crave the food of Egypt, but to obey Him carefully (Exodus 15:26). However, they had travelled for forty years and had dearly missed the foods of Egypt. While on the borders of the promised land of Canaan, they cried out for the foods they missed. They had

An Original Foundation

lost appetite for the manna, the heavenly food directly from God, and demanded flesh food from Moses, their leader. God was displeased but still gave them quail meat. The result was catastrophic. He permitted a great number of them to die as a result of their lust for flesh (Numbers 11:33-34).

> Christ gave to Israel definite instructions in regard to their habits of life, and He assured them, *"The Lord will take away from thee all sickness" (Deut. 7:15).* When they fulfilled the conditions, the promise was verified to them. There was not one feeble person among their tribes. *(Ps. 105:37)*[1]

These were written as lessons for all people. They are conditions to be observed by all who would preserve health. Everyone should learn what these conditions are. The Lord is not pleased with ignorance in regard to His Laws, either natural or spiritual. God, who created the human body, knew and communicated what manner of food should be fuel for the system long before there was a Jew. Principles of health are an integral part of Bible religion. It is imperative that a divine connection exists between sin and disease. However, He still leaves us to make the choice; hence, He says in 3 John 2, *Beloved, I wish above all things that thou mayest prosper and be in health, even as thy soul prospereth.*

God always made a difference between what was food for man – the human body, and what was not. According to Maxwell Ukegbu, "Before the Christian church replaced the Jewish church (Judaism) there was no dispute about what

God's prescribed meal was. When the Christian church started spreading into non-Jewish (Gentile) lands, controversies arose regarding what ritual, and what type of food the non-Jewish Christians ought to practice/eat."[2] More about what followed could be found in the Bible texts of Acts 15:18-29. Further clarification was explained by the Apostle Paul (see Romans 14) due to the religious/social climate and culture of the then known world (Bible lands) at the time. It is important to note that Paul was not disputing God's food laws because it was God's original standard, given to His representatives or ambassadors – the Jewish nation, and to the rest of the world.

For the sake of clarity, it is important to note that the purpose of Peter's vision recorded in Acts 10 was to teach him/other Jewish Christians, who regarded Gentiles as unclean, that everyone was equal and offered salvation in the sight of God. Peter, like Paul and Daniel (Daniel 1:8) knew that he was not to defile his body. Eating clean foods was an established way of life among believers. God identified and named some animals as suitable for human consumption and others as unsuitable. He did not give laws to arbitrarily show control over His creatures, but He gave humanity, before Abraham, laws (including those of which meats are clean or unclean) for their good - "that it might be well" with all who seek to obey Him (Deuteronomy 5:29).[3]

An Original Foundation

The biology of disease was not much understood before and even in the 1800s. The regions of the world struck by the Bubonic plaque, mainly China, Europe, and North Africa, had recovered from its devastating effects, but the role of hygiene, proper eating, rest, and dressing in disease infestation was not quite known, taught, and/or understood. In the great religious awakening of the 1730s, prominent among whom was Jonathan Edwards and George Whitfield, God moved in mysterious ways to enlighten persons to holy living. Many Christians in the west ate pork, smoked cigars, used tea and coffee, and worked restlessly; life expectancy was between 30 and 40 years of age.

In the mid-1800s, while the world was wallowing in pleasure and amusements, disease infestations, the search for cures, for wealth, and for ease, it pleased God, in 1863, to reveal by visions to a young woman, Ellen Gould White, that as the world nears its end, there will be mass perversion of appetite, gluttony, and disease. God already set the stage for human nutrition as seen earlier in Genesis 1:29, 31. He loves us and does not want us to harm ourselves through unhealthful living or practices. He gave these visions, dismantling the biology of disease, so that His servants would not only be sound in spiritual perceptions of the Bible and the great controversy between Christ and Satan in the history of the world, but also so that they would understand the role of physical health and diet in the plan of salvation.

The grand wisdom of God sharing with man is captured in Amos 3:7. God faithfully reveals His secrets to His servants – those who love, respect, honor, and obey/fear Him.

Ellen White's visions on diet, nutrition, lifestyle, and hygiene are found in several books, among which is *Counsels on Diet and Foods,* where (page 81) she penned the following with regards to proper dietary rules and God's original plan for man's diet:

> *"Grains, fruits, nuts, and vegetables constitute the diet chosen for us by our Creator. These foods, prepared in as simple and natural a manner as possible, are the most healthful and nourishing. They impart a strength, a power of endurance, and a vigor of intellect, that are not afforded by a more complex and stimulating diet."*

God warned man against the use of unclean animals. Therefore, further on, in relation to the health hazards of unclean animals, she wrote in *Ministry of Healing* about the pig (pork) as follows:

> *"The tissues of the swine swarm with parasites. Of the swine God said, "It is unclean unto you: ye shall not eat of their flesh, nor touch [314] their dead carcass." Deuteronomy 14:8. This command was given because swine's flesh is unfit for food. Swine are scavengers, and this is the only use they were intended to serve. Never, under any circumstances, was their flesh to be eaten by human beings"* (page 212).

When the Bible says in 2 Corinthians 6:17 not to touch the unclean thing, it meant every aspect of the animal. We can see in these times pork has many by-products used for food and cosmetics. These include gelatin, tallow, pepsin, shortening, lard, tanner's stock, gelatin, chewing gums, pies, beverages, puddings, cheese, and confectionary. It is the responsibility of the shopper to realize that the pig is in the supermarkets and vitamin or mineral shops with different names. Here lies the importance of reading labels. In this century, science affirms what is historically and biblically written concerning the dangers of eating pork. A YouTube presentation titled *STOP EATING PORK!! Swine's Flesh Is Unclean!* cautions on this. You can watch this video at the following location:
https://www.youtube.com/watch?v=uUZkhI8HtEo
It is no wonder, following the Abrahamic/Jewish traditions/customs, the Islamic religion rightly forbids the use of pork as food (see Figure 1).

Evolutionary trends in science, academic thought, social life, religious-political ideologies, diet, and lifestyle left a most serious side effect – the stirring of people's minds towards the worship of the creature – man, instead of the Creator God (Revelation 14:6-12). Some of the most noticeable results of creature worship include multiplications of diseases – psychological, emotional, and

physical conditions – leading to wickedness and a general departure from the principles of wholesome living. Man's inhumanity to man in all forms, shapes, and degrees, deliberate chemical warfare, sowing seeds of discord, deception, and human destruction – these are discussed in the video, *Genetic Roulette, The Gamble of Our Lives*. You can watch this video at the following location:
https://www.youtube.com/watch?v=7sUNxX0OxP8&t=500s

(So, jump to the last chapter. Look at the two-week health challenge. Make your grocery list. Shop within the periphery of the shop where there are live foods. For packaged or processed foods, read the labels carefully. Look at the source, ingredients, and expiration date column. Avoid foods with high sugar or salt content, chemicals and over-fermented, nerve irritating substances like vinegar, alcohol, baking sodas/powder, and other stimulants.)

The point of Peter's vision found in Acts 10, was neither food nor drink. It was a test of faith, trust, loyalty, and belief in the established Word of God about gospel dispersal, about the character of God as no respecter of persons. It was educational, metaphorically using the known to teach an unknown aspect of the gospel. It was essentially about taking the good news of the gospel to the Gentiles. The understanding of the Jews was perverted. Jesus had been with His disciples for about three years. Yet, they did not fully understand His mission. Peter did not fully understand even what the angel was saying. That is why later (Galatians

An Original Foundation

2:11-21), Paul rebuked Peter for acting a double standard when he was with his fellow Jews.

Figure 1. Clean and unclean food

Simple Solutions

When a creature is unclean it cannot be made clean. Yes, the pork, camel, duck, catfish, crab, crayfish, and the likes are unclean. No amount of cleaning can make them clean because they were already created that way by God for a purpose – to give Him glory in the work he has appointed them to do on earth – *scavenging*. They are not for food. Common can be changed. A dirty thing can be cleaned. People – all humanity – were formed in God's image. Likewise, all are offered salvation through Christ. Jews like Peter thought non-Jews were imperfect, common, and could not be cleansed. God often uses the familiar things/proverbs/illustrations/metaphors et cetera, to drive down the message he seeks to be understood.

This section cannot be complete without the mention of alcoholic drinks and wine. The word 'wine' is used for both the freshly harvested juice of the grape and the fermented juice of it. One must always pay close attention to the context. The principle to understanding scripture is found in Isaiah 28:9, 10. God says that wine – grape juice is good and nourishing for the body (Isaiah 68: 5). The wine which Jesus made was not intoxicating. God does not contradict His word. Fermented wine/drink is intoxicating and harmful to the mind. For this reason, He gave laws regarding their use in Leviticus 11 and Deuteronomy 14. God speaks against intoxicating wine in Proverbs 20:1; Isaiah 5:22; 28:1, 7 and more. Moreover, we read from the stories of both parents of

An Original Foundation

Sampson in Judges 13:4, 14 and John the Baptist in Luke 1:15, that an angel of the Lord appeared to these parents at the time of conception to instruct against the use of wine or strong drink. These two men were reformers in their time. Those called to reform society must be temperate, sober, vigilant at all times and must not pollute their bodies with things that excite or irritate the stomach or the nerves or disturb the delicate chemistry of the entire system. Those whose bodies are to be purified as the temple of God must follow the same principles because these stories were written as examples for daily living. Alcohol is useful as medicine, preservative, and cleaning as the need arises. This is the background for Paul's advice to Timothy in 1 Timothy 5:23 and John 2:1-11 where Jesus made the best wine.

God used the story of Daniel and his three Hebrew associates as read in Daniel 1:8-21 to show his distaste of eating and drinking in a manner that is not in harmony with God's divine will for man. From Daniel's experience we see individuals and groups of persons today advocating and practicing a Daniel's diet, and using a 10-day plant-based menu with recipes completely devoid of animal products.

God foresaw that through the ages, there would be pollution of all things, especially flesh based foods, so he warned through inspiration penned in the 1900's as follows:

> *"Flesh was never the best food; but its use is now doubly objectionable, since disease in animals is so rapidly*

increasing...Animals are becoming more and more diseased...Foods that are healthful and life sustaining are to be prepared, so that men and women will not need to eat meat...I am instructed to say that if ever meat eating were safe, it is not safe now...The curse of God is upon the earth, because man has cursed it. The habits and practices of men have brought the earth into such a condition that some other food than animal food must be substituted for the human family. We do not need flesh food at all."[4]

Historical Perspective of Food and Health

Food, we know, is important to human development and lifelong growth. Hence from birth, a child's first instinct is to look for breast milk from the mother or, in the absence of that, any other source of food or drink. Without food, health, good or bad does not exist. Food is important because there are good and bad foods. God in His foreknowledge created and declared all that He made "very good" – Genesis 1:31: *And God saw everything that He had made, and behold, it was very good....* All that God made has a purpose, and so He declared everything good for the purpose for which He created them. Then He spoke to Adam and Eve in Genesis 1:29,30:

> *And God said, Behold, I have given you every herb bearing seed, which is upon the face of all the earth, and every tree, in the which is the fruit of a tree yielding seed; to you it shall be for meat. And to every beast of the earth, and to every fowl of the air, and to everything that creepeth upon the earth, wherein there is life, I have given every green herb for meat: and it was so.*

An Original Foundation

One cannot separate the molecules and atoms in the physical world from their maker who uses spiritual undertones to introduce his workings called 'science.' Thus, when science is separated from religion it creates an imbalance because spiritual and physical nature are interwoven. Medicine becomes powerless if God is not acknowledged as the source of healing.

The journey into the foundations of good health cannot be complete without mentioning the astounding story of Daniel and his three friends in the courts of the great King Nebuchadnezzar of Babylon from 605 to 562 B.C. Here is the story from Daniel 1:3-20:

> *And the king spake unto Ashpenaz the master of his eunuchs, that he should bring certain of the children of Israel, and of the king's seed, and of the princes; children in whom was no blemish, but well favored, and skillful in all wisdom, and cunning in knowledge, and understanding science, and such as had ability in them to stand in the king's palace, and whom they might teach the learning and the tongue of the Chaldeans. And the king appointed them a daily provision of the king's meat, and of the wine which he drank: so, nourishing them three years, that at the end thereof they might stand before the king. Now among these were of the children of Judah, Daniel, Hananiah, Mishael, and Azariah, unto whom the prince of the eunuchs gave names, for he gave unto Daniel the name of Belteshazzar; and to Hananiah, of Shadrach; and to Mishael, of Meshach; and to Azariah, of Abednego. But Daniel purposed in his heart that he would not defile himself with the portion of the king's meat, nor with the wine which he drank. Therefore, he requested of the prince of the eunuchs that he might not defile himself. Now God had brought Daniel into favor and tender love with the prince of the eunuchs. And the prince of the eunuchs said unto Daniel, I fear my lord the king, who*

hath appointed your meat and your drink: for why should he see your faces worse liking than the children which are of your sort? Then shall ye make me endanger my head to the king. Then said Daniel to Melzar, whom the prince of the eunuchs had set over Daniel, Hananiah, Mishael, and Azariah, prove thy servants, I beseech thee, ten days; and let them give us pulse to eat, and water to drink. Then let our countenances be looked upon before thee, and the countenance of the children that eat of the portion of the king's meat: and as thou seest, deal with thy servants. So he consented to them in this matter, and proved them ten days. And at the end of ten days their countenances appeared fairer and fatter in flesh than all the children which did eat the portion of the king's meat. Thus, Melzar took away the portion of their meat, and the wine that they should drink; and gave them pulse. As for these four children, God gave them knowledge and skill in all learning and wisdom: and Daniel had understanding in all visions and dreams. Now at the end of the days that the king had said he should bring them in, then the prince of the eunuchs brought them in before Nebuchadnezzar. And the king communed with them; and among them all was found none like Daniel, Hananiah, Mishael, and Azariah: therefore, stood they before the king. And in all matters of wisdom and understanding, that the king enquired of them, he found them ten times better than all the magicians and astrologers that were in all his realm.

From Daniel's story and example – a desire to glorify God even in food and drink matters, we gather that the many benefits of choosing a healthful lifestyle includes improved cognitive functioning. Clarity of mind in physical and spiritual discernment is promised those who conscientiously and sincerely follow the divine principles of daily living. Interestingly, King Nebuchadnezzar, did not discern and obey God until he was humbled to "eat grass" as an animal for seven years (see Daniel 4:31-34). Until his reasoning was removed and he was struck with temporary insanity, he remained proud and pompous. The eating of *plants* as did Daniel and his friends afforded him an opportunity to have an encounter with heaven, when it dawned on him that the God of Heaven is the true God who deserves his obedience and praise, his "understanding" returned to him. Then God graciously restored him.

Importance of Herbs/Greens

Many herbs and plants share similar characteristics. Plant morphologists (persons who study plant form or structure) work alongside botanists whose work is to analyze plant structures to observe, identify and classify them according to color, shape, size, and other distinguishable characteristics. When wisely used as remedies (dietarily or medicinally), singly or in combination with others, plants are effective in bringing physical and mental relief, restoration, and blessings to the user. In every land, God places varieties and species of annual, perennial and biennial plants, crops, flowers, and weeds suitable to the climactic conditions for food, beauty, and the sustenance of all life forms. See Figure 2 for an example of these varieties.

He teaches its inhabitants that different herbs and parts of plants can be prepared and used in various ways like:

Tea	Salve	Tincture	Poultice
Ointment	Syrups	Infusion	Fomentation
Decoction	Boiling	Fluid extract	

Figure 2. Grains, fruits, nuts, and vegetables

God gave every green plant as food for all the wild animals, the birds in the sky, and the small animals that scurry along the ground—everything that has life, as seen earlier in Genesis. Later on, long after the flood, in Leviticus 11:2-9, God outlined the physical characteristics of creatures that are good to eat and those which are not (clean or unclean). These habits of life were already known to God's people from the beginning but He had to re-iterate them again following their long stay as slaves in Egypt - a period during which they tended to have forgotten their special calling from God, having mixed with cultures who practiced the consumption of things forbidden by God. He had warned

An Original Foundation

them earlier as they exited Egypt that He was in charge of their every aspect of life and that a promise of good health awaited them if they practiced obedience. This is seen from Exodus 15:26, in which the Lord assured them saying,

> *If thou wilt diligently hearken to the voice of the LORD thy God, and wilt do that which is right in his sight, and wilt give ear to His commandments, and keep all His statutes, I will put none of these diseases upon thee, which I have brought upon the Egyptians: for I am the LORD that healeth thee.*

The Lord said He would take away all sickness from them (Deuteronomy 7:15). God on His own part so verified the promise as they fulfilled the conditions, so much so that it was recorded in Psalm 105:37, that there was not one feeble person among their tribes.

Today, scientific discovery and study of ancient mummies of Egypt show that the DNA - *(Deoxyribonucleic acid – one of two types of molecules that encode genetic information.)* of these bodies still show the diseases that killed them (see Figure 3 for a picture of an Egyptian mummy). They examined bone samples and non-rehydrated mummified soft tissues to arrive at their health history, disease, age, as well as the cause of death.[5]

> *"Many of the diseases which cause problems in today's society afflicted Egyptian populations. These include tuberculosis, malaria and schistosomiasis. In drawing upon examples of each beginning with the bacterial, a high proportion of mummified corpses are individuals who died from tuberculosis."*[6]

Figure 3. Egyptian mummy

So, food is important because it nourishes and determines the wellbeing of all the cells, tissues, and organs of our body which, the Bible says, is the temple of the Holy Spirit, who quickens our movement in all directions of living.

> Acts 17:28: *For in Him we live, and move, and have our being; as certain also of your own poets have said, for we are also His offspring.*

What we eat affects the nature of our behavior and human interactions for good or for evil. Food is equally important because control of it goes a long way to determine individual ability to set boundaries for do's and don'ts in life. In health care there is a focus on 'numbers' (blood pressure, sugar, etc.), but there is no number that is responsible for any disease, be it cardiovascular or other. The basic and singular factor responsible for disease is what is fed into the body – the food.

Disease and Lifespan

God had an ideal for man whom He made in His image, so He had an ideal diet for his nourishment because what he eats directly impacts his body, physically and spiritually. As earlier seen in Genesis 1:29, God gave them instructions to eat fruit, nuts, seeds and grains. He later added vegetables and herbs after the fall (Genesis 3:18) and flesh foods followed, but not without 'side effects' (Genesis 2:15). Man's lifespan began to decrease after the fall and introduction of the flesh of animals in the diet. The average American's life span is only about 78 years compared to others in some parts of Europe and Asia. In fact, it is scientifically proven that people who practice vegetarianism attain a life span much longer or different from those whose diet contains meat, as evidenced in the articles found in the *National Geographic Magazines* of October 27, 2005,[7] November 24, 2010,[8] and August 14, 2013.[9] It is also possible that the lifespan got shortened due to genetics and moral declension after the fall. Here is a stunning description of the reduction of lifespan as an aftermath of sin.

> *"After the flood the people ate largely of animal food. God saw that the ways of man were corrupt, and that he was*

> *disposed to exalt himself proudly against his Creator and to follow the inclinations of his own heart. And He permitted that long-lived race to eat animal food to shorten their sinful lives. Soon after the flood the race began to rapidly decrease in size, and in length of years."*[10]

In the long run, it is not much about the *eating* of the 'fruit' as it was of the *disobedience* in Eden.

According to recent statistics, the average American lives 78 years. Ellen White wrote that in comparison, men before the flood lived many hundreds of years and were considered youth at age one hundred.

> *"Those long-lived men had sound minds in sound bodies.... They came upon the stage of action from the ages of sixty to one hundred years, about the time those who now live the longest have acted their part in their little short lifetime and have passed off the stage."*[11]

The Bible stories recorded most of the patriarchs as having died peacefully in their sleep after a long useful and productive life, un-ravaged by debilitating disease. See Figures 4, 5, 6, and 7 for depictions of decreasing lifespans and size reduction.

Notice the drastic reduction from after Noah. Note also that Enoch did not live out his years on earth but was translated/taken to heaven as an example of those whose lives will be pure on earth and who will be alive at the time of Jesus' second coming. Such will not taste death but will be translated alive to heaven, just like Enoch (1 Corinthians 15:51-52 and 1 Thessalonians 4:13-18). The Creator blessed

An Original Foundation

man with a tremendous life force so much that even after sin entered, the patriarchs lived for nearly 1000 years. However, after the flood, lifespan rapidly declined and human height also began to decrease.

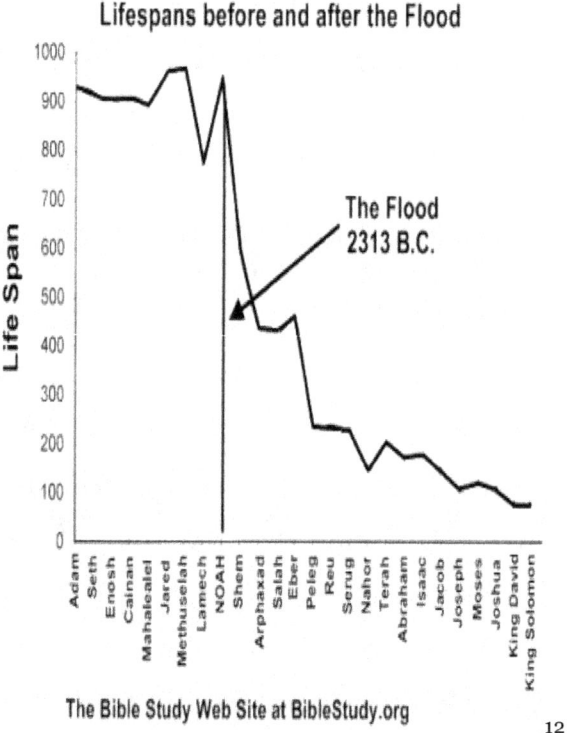

Figure 4. Lifespans before and after Noah's flood

It was God's original design that man thrive on plant-based diet and enjoy life to the fullest. One may argue that there is a relationship between aging, genetics, and lifespan.

Simple Solutions

Due to the presence of evil and disobedience on the earth, sadly, God declared a decrease in lifespan. One can safely deduce, therefore, that the presence of sin (evil) altered human genetics, hence the change in lifespan.

Figure 5. Ten generations before the flood

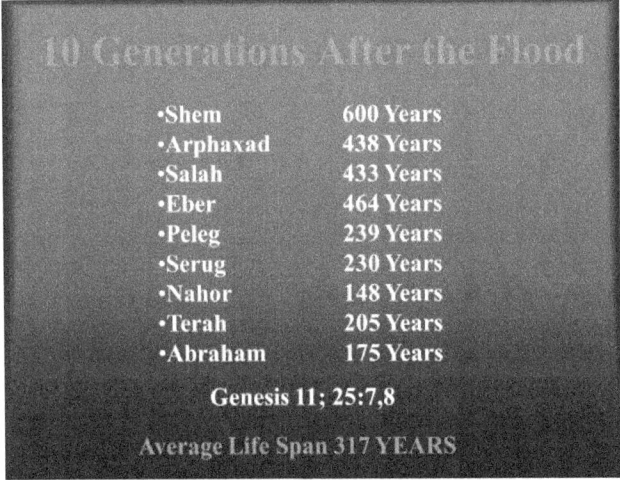

Figure 6. Ten generations after the flood

An Original Foundation

Figure 7. Dramatic size reduction.

(Source: *Your Bible and You* by Arthur Maxwell -1959 Edition. Page 268-269)

> Psalm 90:9-10: *For all our days are passed away in thy wrath: we spend our years as a tale that is told. The days of our years are threescore years and ten; and if by reason of strength they be fourscore years, yet is their strength labor and sorrow; for it is soon cut off, and we fly away.*

Yet, the Creator himself made provision for the sustenance of the race by establishing hygienic and dietary laws. Thus, while on the way to Canaan, He fed the children of Israel with manna (Exodus 16). Later, they grumbled and wanted flesh food (Numbers 11). God permitted them to have it but it brought more harm than good to them at the end. They died by the thousands. Here God taught the evil of unbelief, gluttony, and dependence on flesh food instead of dependence on Him; and very importantly, the seriousness of obedience to the Sabbath commandment (Exodus 16:22-35).

Eating plant-based is a surer way of disease avoidance or disorder eradication in the body. Disorder is actually what happens when the normal bodily function and structure in a living organism becomes internally and progressively altered, leading to a feeling of pain and discomfort. A definition of disease, which I find very practical and applicable to all human condition, is this:

> *"Disease is an effort of nature to free the system from conditions that result from a violation of the laws of health"*[13].

Thus, disease can be viewed as a vehicle, a friendly reminder about something wrong in the system, a friendly attempt of nature (God) to restore the body to health – the health that was lost in disregarding His laws, which govern our physical bodies. The last four chapters of Deuteronomy center on the results of obedience – obey and be saved or disobey and be lost. Furthermore, Mrs. White writes,

> *"It is a sin to be sick, for all sickness is the result of transgression."*[14]

Scientific research in healthful living is proving the importance of plants, nuts, seeds, grains, and vegetables as potent weapons to disarm disease. Nature knows best how to heal itself, given the natural food that is bio-identical to human structure. The human body, just like other elements of creation, is governed by laws of health. Any foods or chemical introductions short of the natural sooner or later predispose the body to inflammation, dysfunction, disease, and eventual tissue decay because the natural course of bodily living has been violated. The body is equipped with channels of elimination to help eliminate any abnormal condition which might exist as toxic waste in the blood. Toxins get to the body through the air, water, food, drug medications, and household cleaning and body grooming products. Some of these can be carefully avoided, while others cannot be avoided. When toxins are not expelled, they are stored in the body as fat and might lead to weight gain. The body's seven channels (organs) of toxic waste elimination are the blood, colon, kidney, liver, lymph, lungs, and skin – the skin/mucous membranes being the largest.

Evolution of Eating Patterns

It was not always the practice for people to eat three meals per day. By the beginning of the Middle Ages, a number of circumstances influenced eating times. One of these was monastic life, due to the times of the morning Mass and observation of other religious rituals. Historians chronicle that the 17th century (1601 – 1700) marked the beginnings of eating breakfast – a practice which today, has been proven to promote mental alertness, better metabolism, trimness, behavior modification, decrease of hunger, prevention of blood sugar hikes, improvement of memory function, weight control, and more. Eating habits were also influenced by the industrial revolution (1700s into the late 1800s), and into the mid-19th century, when the working class increased. Work started early, and most people started to eat breakfast before going to work. Within this period, John Harvey Kellogg, (a Seventh-day Adventist physician, health reformer, and superintendent [1876] of the Health Reform Institute in Battle Creek, Michigan) revolutionized breakfast, making it easier to eat the grains, as he created the first corn flakes in the world. A new industry and wave of breakfast, which attracted government promotion, was born to the world.

Another event that affected eating habits and times was World War II. Years after the effects of the ravages and scarcity created by war, necessity became the mother of a plethora of inventions. More choices of foods became available, including refined and processed types. Over time, it was not only eating breakfast that became popular, but a midday meal – lunch, became a practice. Towards the late 1800s, the emergence of artificial lighting and working hours affected eating patterns among the working and social classes in the cities and towns. The availability of mass-produced industrialized foods and the work ethic popularized the eating of a third meal – dinner. Thus, by the late 19th century, (1870s to early 1900s) people were eating three meals a day. Then in 1986, the microwave oven was born, thus, introducing a considerable degree of ease to cooking and eating. Some opine that the industrialized world enjoyed a better bill of health before the advent of many modern inventions of ease and the three meals a day eating pattern.[15]

Vegetarian, Vegan, or Health Reformer

Vegetarian

The American Dietetic Association confirms that a well-planned vegetarian diet provides adequate nutrition at all states of life. However, in planning meals, balance of nutrients, acids and alkaline forming foods must be considered. People who used to practice vegetarianism abstained from eating meat and by-products of animals used as food. Vegetarian eating may be adopted for personal health reasons, or (for Bible believers) a disbelief in taking life or in animal suffering. Some people adopt the vegetarian lifestyle for ethical reasons. By the 1830s the word vegetarian was already in existence and according to the dictionary, vegetarianism was associated with Seventh-day Adventists – considered a religious conservative group who were noted for promoting the temperance movement and non-alcohol use. They still promote the same principles wherever they live. Vegetarians eat lots of vegetables and fruits. This is because they obtain all the basic nutrients, minerals, vitamins, and antioxidants to maintain good health, from plants. By the use of a meat free diet, they avoid animal fat and are free from polluting their bodies from the hormones and antibiotics from farmed-animals, and toxins from even the free-range animals.

In 1847, the British Vegetarian Society was founded. However, prior to this founding, the light on hygienic living and reform was gaining momentum on the east coast of America as part of the great religious awakening, when many Christians preached and looked forward to the second advent/return of Jesus Christ. There were health reformers in many denominations. In support of the spirit of the times, we find this account from David Paulson, M.D., who wrote in the *Signs of the Times*:

> *"Nearly all great religious reformers were also health reformers - John Wesley (Methodist), Sylvester Graham (Presbyterian), and Charles Grandison Finney, (founder of Oberlin College of the Congregational Church). Like all reformers, they met with opposition; for remember, if you have no opposition you are no reformer. No doubt God*

> *committed those vital health and temperance truths to the stewardship of these three great denominations, first of all because they needed them, and second because the world needed them as part of their preparation to enable them to live through the perils of the last days, when sickness and suffering shall become almost universal."*[16]

Graham promoted a vegetarian diet and was noted for his Graham bread and crackers. Sabbath-keeping Adventists were privileged to have among them a messenger through whom God gave visions about hygienic reforms, temperance, and general living. These Sabbath-keeping Adventists, who later became known as Seventh-day Adventists, were guided through the inspiration and ministry of Ellen G. White (nee Harmon) to learn that humans were originally designed to eat nuts, seeds, grains, fruits and vegetables (plant-based) and no animal products of any kind. Through her visions arose a mission to educate and prepare a sick world for the second return of Jesus Christ. Dietetic reform was practiced by many before Mrs. White was shown visions, which clarified many of the issues of that age and brought a rather religious hue to the reforms. Here is a short narration found on the book, *How to Live*, compiled by James and Ellen White and others in 1865:

> *"Elder J. H. Waggoner writing in the same number of the Review and Herald, the Church organ, said, "We do not profess to be pioneers in the general principles of the health reform. The facts on which this movement is based have been elaborated, in a great measure, by reformers, physicians, and writers on physiology and hygiene, and so*

may be found scattered through the land. But we do claim that by the method of God's choice it has been more clearly and powerfully unfolded and is thereby producing an effect which we could not have looked for from any other means."

"As mere physiological and hygienic truths, they might be studied by some at their leisure, and by others laid aside as of little consequence, but when placed on a level with the great truths of the third angels message by the sanction, and authority of God's spirit, and so declared to be the means whereby a weak people be made strong to overcome, and our diseased bodies cleansed and fitted for translation, then it comes to us as an essential part of present truth, to be received with the blessing of God, or rejected at our own peril."

"The work of health reform is the Lord's means for lessening suffering in our world and for purifying His church. Counsels on Health," 443.

"The Lord has been sending us line upon line and if we reject these principles, we are not rejecting the messenger who teaches them, but the One who has given us the principles." Counsels on Health, 48."[17]

It is largely because Seventh-day Adventists (SDA) made light of their call, deviated from their assignment to educate the world, that much disease and suffering which add to the deplorable condition of man exists. If SDAs trusted and practiced the testimonies given to them since the mid-1800s with regards to how to live, the advancement of confusing, non-sustainable varieties of diets – (Atkins, Zone, Ketogenic, Vegetarian, Vegan, Western, Mediterranean, Weight Watchers, Raw food, South Beach, etc.) should not have existed.

An Original Foundation

Vegan

Donald Watson is credited with coining the name 'vegan' in 1944. He co-founded the Vegan Society of England. This was founded on the premise that man should not be exploiting animals and so must not use dairy. Since the 2000s, more restaurants and health food stores offer vegan foods, and many more persons from all walks of life, including athletes, have embraced veganism and raw eating. However, strict vegans extend their desire for non-exploitation of animals to non-use of animal clothing including fur, belts, hats etc. In contemporary society, many promote a vegetarian lifestyle (particularly creationists – Bible believers) because it stands close to the original diet which God prescribed for humans. Other vegan groups promote their ideal of respecting animal life by avoiding cruelty to them. In the book, *Patriarchs and Prophets,* Ellen White writes against the abuse of animals:

> *"He who will abuse animals because he has them in his power is both a coward and a tyrant. A disposition to cause pain, whether to our fellow men or to the brute creation, is satanic. Many do not realize that their cruelty will ever be known, because the poor dumb animals cannot reveal it. But could the eyes of these men be opened, as were those of Balaam, they would see an angel of God standing as a witness, to testify against them in the courts above. A record goes up to heaven, and a day is coming when judgment will be pronounced against those who abuse God's creatures."*[18]

In fact, the full message from that passage is that no meat/flesh will be used by those who truly love the Creator.

Health Reformer

The health reform here referred to is different from the government policy of health care delivery in the USA or elsewhere. Health reform is just what the name implies – simplicity of diet and the practice of temperance in daily living. A health reformer, therefore, is one who practices a reformed health/lifestyle. Health reform is God's means of lessening human suffering. The message and practice of health reform is one introduced into the Seventh-day Adventist church in the 1800s through the special ministry and visions of Ellen G. White. She was shown that of all temporal possessions, health is the most precious and that the diet must be such as should bring the individual to a position of ability to accomplish the greatest amount of good in their body and in the lives of others. She was shown that those (meaning Sabbath keepers) to whom the light about health reform has been given, and who are looking forward to the second coming of Jesus, should manifest greater interest in health reform. Her position was that the object of the teaching and practice of health reform is the revelation of the way of eternal life.[19] Such a position requires change from self-destroying habits and compliance to the divine will by living in accordance to the laws God has implanted in man so that the human constitution – biological make up – does not break down prematurely.

Health reform involves the belief and practice of the preservation of both physical and moral health, helping the human agent combat disease by using simple methods of treatment that God has provided. Such includes Christian temperance in all things, how to prepare food, and how and when to eat or drink for the preservation of health in accordance with the moral and physical laws given to humans by God the Creator. Therefore, health reformers are what Seventh-day Adventists were originally meant to be. They were to be persons who are conscious and zealous of reforming lifestyle by abstaining from any article of food or habit which is injurious to the health of the human machinery. Seventh-day Adventists were called to constantly advocate a wholesome, healthful, nourishing diet - plainly presented – to teach a way of living the abundant life. Said Mrs. White,

> *"Knowledge must be gained in regard to how to eat, and drink, and dress so as to preserve health.... When premature death is the result of our violation of nature's law, we bring sorrow and suffering to others.... Then, are we not, in the worst sense, transgressors of God's law?"*[20]

The true Christian believes and sees value in the foundation and pillars of the Christian faith, about which the heavenly sanctuary is central. The central theme of the Bible, the theme about which every other in the entire book

Simple Solutions

clusters, is the redemption plan, the restoration in the human soul of the image of God. One such pillar states:

"The correct understanding of the ministration in the heavenly sanctuary is the foundation of our faith."[21]

It's all about the plan of how to raise humans from sin unto salvation – a plan of salvation in which food plays a key role in the body temple (sanctuary), since food affects the physical, mental, and emotional states of being.

One might choose to be 'vegan' but not a health reformer. Health reform must be adopted from a sense of duty to self and others. Consider, in Table 1, some of the outstanding differences in the two ways of living.

Table 1. Contrast Between Vegans and Health Reformers

Vegans May:	BUT Health Reformers Avoid:
<ul><li>Not eat at regular times.</li><li>Snack</li><li>Drink alcohol or eat food with alcohol in it</li><li>Drink coffee, energy drinks, and non-herbal tea</li><li>Drink soda & diet soda</li><li>Drink with their meals</li><li>Eat chocolate</li><li>Eat more than 2-3 kinds of food at a meal</li></ul>	<ul><li>Eating between meals</li><li>The use of alcohol or eating food with alcohol in it; alcohol destroys brain cells; damages the liver and more.</li><li>Drinking coffee, energy drinks, and tea, or using tobacco, b/c they affect the nervous system and more</li><li>Drinking soda & diet soda b/c they disturb the nervous system and more</li><li>Drinking with their meals because it dilutes the</li></ul>

An Original Foundation

<ul><li>Eat potato chips, fried corn chips, fried potato chips</li><li>Eat right before bed</li><li>Fry their food or cook with any grease</li><li>Mix fruit & vegetables at a meal</li><li>Use baking soda & baking powder</li><li>Use black & white pepper or hot sauces in their food</li><li>Use condiments like ketchup, pickles, vinegar</li><li>Use artificial food coloring</li><li>Use tobacco</li><li>Use nutmeg, cinnamon, and allspice</li><li>Use vinegar or anything with vinegar in it</li><li>**Not be a Christian – one who believes and follows the footsteps of Jesus Christ as revealed in the Bible**</li></ul>	digestive juices, causing food to rot in the stomach <ul><li>Eating chocolate - because it often contains toxic substances that lead to many health problems</li><li>Eating more than 2-3 kinds of food at a meal because such combinations cause fermentation in the stomach</li><li>Eating fried corn chips, fried potato chips b/c it raises the risk of diseases including diabetes, high blood pressure, etc.</li><li>Snacking b/c it disturbs digestion time, causing fermentation in the stomach, poisons the blood, kills appetite, and leads to weight gain and obesity</li><li>Eating late in the evening or after 3 pm because digestive enzymes and certain hormones are slower after this time</li><li>Frying their food or cooking with any animal grease/fat because it poisons the blood, raises the risk for heart disease, etc.</li><li>**Mixing fruits & vegetables at a meal because such practice can cause harm for persons with a weak digestive system**</li><li>Using baking soda & baking powder because they insidiously poison the blood;</li></ul>

	disturb the PH balance of the stomach
	• Using black & white pepper, cayenne, other hot peppers, hot sauce, nutmeg, cinnamon, allspice, etc. in their food b/c they tear the lining of the stomach and make the blood feverish
	• Using vinegar b/c it poisons the blood, causes anemia, disturbs digestion; platelets, etc.
	• Using artificial food colors because it could cause, allergies; affect transmitters in the brain, and lead to hyperactivity in children.
	• The true health reformer is a Christian who believes in and practices the teachings of the Bible as recorded in Isaiah 58; obeys *ALL* the Ten Commandments (*not some*) and follows the principles of the kingdom as revealed in the life and teachings of Jesus Christ.

Seventh-day Adventist Perspectives on Food and Nutrition

Seventh-day Adventists recommend a vegetarian diet. The church has advocated a healthy lifestyle since its organization in 1863. The emphasis on health of body and

An Original Foundation

mind stands out as one of the church's fundamental beliefs, noted in *Seventh-day Adventists Believe*:

> "Because our bodies are the temples of the Holy Spirit, we are to care for them intelligently. Along with adequate exercise and rest, we are to adopt the most healthful diet possible and abstain from the unclean foods identified in the scriptures. Since alcoholic beverages, tobacco, and the irresponsible use of drugs and narcotics are harmful to our bodies, we are to abstain from them as well."[22]

According to Buettner, SDAs are known for living long, healthy lives and for promoting a natural vegetarian diet rich in fruits, grains, nuts, and vegetables. It is recommended that the diet include a wise use of nuts, whole grain breads, seeds, cereals, pastas, fresh vegetables, fruits, and legumes. Some also advocate a moderate inclusion of low-fat dairy products such as milk, yogurt, cheese, and eggs. Since the 1950s, research has been done on the Adventist lifestyle. As a result, it is believed that the length of life and quality of health enjoyed by SDA vegetarians is due in particular to the consumption of whole grains, fruits and vegetables as well as the avoidance of meat, alcohol, coffee, and tobacco.[23]

As a church, SDA's are encouraged to follow a vegetarian diet, which demonstrates that, followed closely, it lowers the risks of major diseases. The church follows the inspired writings given in regard to health and well-being through the writings of Ellen G. White. Her counsel mandates health education and a healing ministry as an essential partner for successful evangelizing. The media, such as the *Christian Science Monitor*, publicly acknowledges the Adventist standpoint on health, and encourages the public to learn from Adventists. The article highlights and praises holistic education as practiced by SDA institutions of learning, embracing the spiritual, the health-physical, and the emotional aspects of man.[24] It is the church's stand that the natural remedies, being nutrition, exercise, water, sunshine, temperance, air, rest and trust in Divine power (NEWSTART), are principles of good health. The church also holds that these simple remedies are God's original plan for man, and this stand continues to hold global appeal.[25] Moreover, Adventists link their health and dietary reform message with evangelism as seen in Matthew 28 and Revelation 14:6-12.

It is expected that Seventh-day Adventists worldwide are united in their belief system and with one voice, focus on teaching, upholding and coaching the public through community efforts, on how to live dietary and holistic reformed lifestyles. However, it seems in some ways that SDA leadership are not totally in consonance with the ideals – 'God's plan' as presented by Ellen White. They seem to stand on the side of the United States Department of Agriculture (USDA) food pyramid. According to the church's position statement on vegetarian diets in the *Adventist*

An Original Foundation

Report, as cited by Nedley, dairy products are endorsed, whereas medical science continues to find and confirm that eating a variety of plant-based diet supplies all essential amino acids the body needs.[26] Understandably, there is not one single vegetarian eating pattern. The church apparently wants to be seen as fair, giving people choices. The American Dietetic Association (ADA), as cited by Nedley, said in 2008:

> *"It is the position of the American Dietetic Association that vegetarian diets are healthful and nutritionally adequate when appropriately planned."*[27]

> *"Some advocate dairy for the sake of calcium for the bones, but it is also found that the human body can subsist on calcium from common green foods instead of risking bone degeneration caused by mal-absorption of milk protein."*[28]

There are parts of the world where people do not use dairy 'milk' in their diet. Their calcium is derived from nuts, fruits, and locally grown vegetables. Animal and fatty products were not in God's original plan to sustain the human race. There is a wealth of research in favor of complete detachment from animal proteins for spiritual, emotional, and physical wellness. This writer appreciates how Colbert treats the issue of fatty foods:

> *"The fat we eat overtaxes our bodies with thick sludge-like, yellowish brown material that encrusts the inside of our arteries, forms plaque, fattens our bodies and shortens our lives."*[29]

Campbell says that animal protein increases the acid load in the body, making our blood and tissues more acidic.[30] Meat eating is associated with different body weaknesses and illnesses. SDAs will do well to stay on their prophetic calling and in tune with the Bible and writings of Ellen White. She warned in the mid-1800s:

> *"The liability to take disease is increased ten-fold by meat eating."*[31]

The psalmist, King David, says in Psalm 67:2:

> *That thy way may be known upon earth, thy saving health among all nations.*

It is this life and health message that was committed to all who keep the commandments of God to declare, live, and teach the world. It is a message that purifies, purges, and frees the mind to comprehend and understand the truth of God's word. Ministers of the gospel were and still are to deepen both knowledge and practice in the health message. Said she,

> *"Ministers and people must make greater advancement in the work of reform. They should commence without delay to correct their wrong habits of eating, drinking, dressing, and working...Ministers should be ensamples..."*[32]

On this premise, and many more revelations pertaining to reformation in daily living, she wrote:

> *"If Seventh-day Adventists practiced what they professed to believe, if they were sincere health reformers, they would indeed be a spectacle to the world, to angels and to men."*[33]

Since it would appear that Seventh-day Adventists have not committed wholly to this calling, the deplorable health crisis, the global burden of disease for the most part,

is an indictment of Seventh-day Adventists who have failed to live and share a divine vision; a comprehensive, wholistic and sustainable message of life and health, healing, restoration and reformation unto salvation; a message which, when well understood, bears a total picture of what it means to **live** and to **die.** See the video – *Tell the World* at the following location:
https://www.youtube.com/watch?v=nH2roJ5VbL4&t=658s

Contribution of the "China Doctor"

A notable and significant contribution to food and nutrition was made by Dr. Harry W. Miller. He and William J. Morse were among the many people who pioneered in bringing soy foods to America. They were described as men of 'great vision, dedication, and perseverance'. According to an unpublished manuscript, "Dr. Miller, the well-known "China Doctor" (after his biography by that title), was a world-famous missionary doctor and surgeon, and founder of more than 15 Seventh-day Adventist hospitals around the world. He was one of those unique individuals who was both a dreamer and a doer. He inspired almost everyone who knew him. Like W. J. Morse, he considered it his personal responsibility to awaken the West to the great potential of the soybean and soy foods. (But where Morse was interested in soybean agronomy, livestock feeding, and food, Miller was interested only in food uses and actively opposed the feeding of soybeans to livestock to produce flesh foods). Dr. Miller can also be considered the founder of the modern soymilk renaissance in Asia.[34]

Chapter 2

Food and the Body

"To eat is a necessity, but to eat intelligently is an art."
La Rochefoucauld

Proteins build and repair body tissues. They are found in meat products (cheese, eggs, milk), legumes (bean, whole grains, nuts) fish, and poultry. All human protein needs are available from plant sources. Consumption of animal protein is eating 'second-hand protein,' whereas proteins can be obtained directly from plants. From global perspectives, dairy milk is considered an important source of protein and especially calcium. The *American Journal of Clinical Nutrition (AJCN)* in a 2001-2002 survey on dairy milk reports:

> *"Milk is the most economical source of many nutrients, especially calcium, potassium, and magnesium, and that milk and milk products have protective effects for bone disorders, Insulin Resistance Syndrome (IRS), and stroke; therefore, calcium should be consumed in adequate quantities to meet demands for growth and obligatory losses."*[35]

Countering this view, Dr. Neal Nedley opines that more calcium is not what is needed for improving the bone health of Americans – or anyone else for that matter. He states that the more protein in the diet the greater the risk of osteoporosis.[36] Moreover, many scientists and critics of animal protein implicate all dairy and other products made from milk: non-fat milk, low-fat milk, buttermilk, cheese, cottage cheese, yogurt, ice cream, whey, kefir, and butter as products that share a similar nutritional profile. For this reason, they all (plus or minus the fat, protein, and sugar) contribute to a wide range of health challenges.

Walter Veith, PhD, professor of nutrition and international lecturer, confirms the ill effects of the products from the dairy industry on a YouTube video titled *Dairy, Casein and Diabetes,* and another presentation titled *Dairy Milk and Health Dangers: Udderly Amazing."* You can watch both at the following location: https://www.youtube.com/watch?v=E4EeK1n4JJE

Whether low or high fat, milk is just unsafe. The milk for baby calves is just more suitable for them than for humans. As Dr. Colin Campbell, American biochemist and Professor Emeritus of Nutritional Biochemistry at Cornell University puts it,

> *"We live in a time when consuming 'low-fat' foods are synonymous with "healthy."*

Low fat technology is drastically advanced to include not just dairy, but other foods, and this might be a deception. Dr. Campbell notes:

> "...beef, pork, lamb and veal consumption is decreasing, while lower-fat chicken, turkey, and fish consumption is increasing. In fact, by consuming more poultry and fish, people have been increasing their total meat intake to record-high amounts, while trying (and largely failing) to reduce their fat intake."[37]

Globally, current literature on animal protein sounds the alarm that since both dairy and meat products available to the public remain deficient in fiber, iron, or calcium, it becomes more advisable to lean towards plant-based nutrition. Moreover, it is observed that 1 in 6 dairy cows suffer from clinical mastitis – a disease of the udder, resulting in having pus in dairy milk.[38] This definitely makes milk objectionable on the dining table. From the environmental point of view, the *Journal of Environmental and Public Health* observes:

> "Promoting increased consumption of plant-based foods is a recommended strategy to reduce human impact on the environment and is also now recognized as a potential strategy to reduce the high rates of some chronic diseases such as cardiovascular disease and certain cancers."[39]

In response to the relationship of disease to the quality of food to the diet, there is a growing awareness in many countries around the world of the importance of eating natural foods, prepared carefully to enhance digestion. Furthermore, Ellen G. White, author and American

Christian pioneer, had admonished, through inspiration, that eggs and healthy fowls were good enough for the table in her day but that time was coming when they would become most objectionable sources of food, including meat. She said that reformation of diet should be progressive:

> "As disease in animals' increases, the use of milk and eggs will become more and more unsafe. An effort should be made to supply their place with other things that are healthful and inexpensive."[40]

She advocated that a gradual change be made from meat-eating to a completely plant-based diet:

> "The simple grains, fruits of the trees, vegetables, have all the nutritive properties necessary to make good blood. This a flesh diet cannot do."[41]

There is a general world view that without 'meat' in the diet, the individual will be protein deficient and disease prone. Making the term 'protein' synonymous with meat is what I would consider a 'protein myth.' In his book, *International Meat Crisis*, Vance Ferrell wrote about the fatal degenerative disease, scrapie, which kills cattle, sheep, and goats, and has also been killing humans in Britain and the USA. Persons who ate the infected meats (protein) since the 1970s have been suffering from debilitating degenerative brain diseases from both the scrapie and "mad cow disease" (bovine spongiform encephalopathy). Dr. Stanley Benjamin Prusiner, an American **neurologist** and **biochemist** won a Nobel prize in 1997 for his research and discovery of prions.

In humans, the disease is called the Creutzfeldt–Jakob disease. It attacks the nervous systems of its victims. This damaged and infectious protein from the infected animal, called a prion, causes chronic wasting. It does not matter whatever part of the infected animal is consumed, the infectious agent is contained in the meat, from cells to the tissues, throughout the body, including blood. Following is a link for more information on prions:
https://www.youtube.com/watch?v=t9SojZv7hMI

For years since the discovery of this disease, people in various parts of the western world and beyond have been harboring it, as many cattle used for food have been infected. Worse still, some of these infected animals get slaughtered and ground up, feces and intestines included, and fed to their living colleagues, who also become "mad." Cows, naturally vegetarians, are fed with chicken waste, growth hormones, and steroids. Such meats become food on the tables of thousands of people. Over time, waste matter builds up in the brain, mad cow disease results, brain cells die, cognition dwindles, a diagnosis of Alzheimer's disease and or dementia – people losing their brains due to the consumption of meat, milk, and other animal products - is often the result. It all means that meat ground up for food could contain components of dead, diseased, dying, disabled animals, or other toxic substances. Generally indicating the

Food and the Body

harrowing condition of today's animals killed for food, the following quotations need to be clearly pondered:

Compare these statements written over 100 years apart:

Ellen G. White – 1900; 1870; 1901

Animals are becoming more and more diseased, and it will not be long until animal food will be discarded by many besides Seventh-day Adventists. Foods that are healthful and life sustaining are to be prepared, so that men and women will not need to eat meat...The very animals whose flesh you eat, are frequently so diseased that, if left alone, they would die of themselves; but while the

Vance Ferrell – 2001

In 1906, Upton Sinclair wrote: "This is no fairy story and no joke. The meat would be shoveled into carts, and the man who did the shoveling would not trouble himself to lift out a rat even when he saw one. — There were things that went into the sausage in comparison with which a poisoned rat was a tidbit" (Upton Sinclair, The Jungle, p. 135) ... If the animal is in bad shape but still can walk, it is sent to the slaughterhouse. If it is too breath of life is in them, they are killed and brought to market. You take directly into your system humors and poison of the worst kind, and yet you realize it not... Worldly physicians cannot account for the rapid increase of disease among the human family. But we know that much of this suffering is caused by the eating of dead flesh...[42]

sick to walk or has already died of disease, it is sent to the rendering plant to be turned into pellets to be fed to livestock... At the rendering plant, the whole animal (including the intestines and the manure in it) is ground up and turned into "high-protein pellets." These are then sold as "animal feed" to cattle, sheep, pig, chicken, and turkey ranchers. [43]

The cause of disease may not always be immediately known, but a careful examination of the articles of food consumed, the combination and timing of it might not be too far from the cause. At the same time, examining aspects of the individual's lifestyle which is out of harmony with the laws of nature may offer a clue.

Carbohydrates

Carbohydrates constitute the main energy source for the body. Eating the right or complex carbohydrates will help to sustain energy, steady blood sugar, regulate mood, and guarantee slow but regulated absorption. Carbohydrates are the primary fuel for the brain. Components of good or complex carbohydrates must include protein and fiber.

Carbohydrates are obtained from grains (breads), fruits, starchy vegetables, and sugars. From the carbohydrate foods we eat, the body makes its glucose. The liver and muscle tissues store glycogen, which the body can use if it runs out of glucose, and if glycogen is low, the body converts protein and fats into glucose. These natural safety precautions are provisions made to enable the body to continually have a stable supply of blood sugar for brain and other body functions.

Any blood sugar drops are reactions to the quality of food eaten, like highly refined carbohydrates. One of the major culprits is sugar from sugar cane or sugar beets, otherwise known as Sucrose. It contains no fiber, which is needed to break food down in the stomach. A better and healthier less concentrated form of sugars are found in natural foods like fruits, vegetables, and whole grains because, these have fiber. Thus, Stitt adds that the whiteness of white sugar confirms that it has no nutritional value but delivers only calories.[44] Eating more of these refined foods starves the cells in the body, thus causing a feeling of weakness and constant demand for food that is rather less nourishing.

Carbohydrates are not enemies, but friends when eaten the right way and at the right times. The issue is not to follow a menu, food, or caloric measurement of 'carbs' or supplements that might become cumbersome, but to understand the needs of the body, and feed it adequately and in a timely manner. Ellen White wrote in 1876:

> *"After the regular meal is eaten, the stomach should be allowed to rest for five hours. Not a particle of food should be introduced into the stomach till the next meal. In this interval the stomach will perform its work and will then be in a condition to receive more food."*[45]

Thus, the importance of eating at regular times makes a difference in wellness. The body is given a particular rhythm within which to function optimally, and those who obey these principles enjoy a sense and feeling of wellbeing. Today, sick persons (diabetics) are often instructed to eat between meals – to indulge on nuts or fruits or confectionary with portion control, to eat at nearly all hours. Such, according to inspired writings – now supported by science – destroys the digestive organs and ruins the system by working against the natural laws of health. In addition to eating the wrong articles of food, this is why, they seldom get completely healed![46]

Fats

Fats are also sources of energy which increase the absorption of fat-soluble vitamins that help to facilitate growth. The best sources are from raw nuts, seeds, avocados, and those oils cold pressed out from foods with high natural oil content. Such products, like olive oil, are less likely damaged by heat from extraction. They are not hydrogenated like margarine and do not have preservatives and chemical, stabilizers and flavorings. Fats provide aroma, taste, and texture to food.

Fats from animal protein are highly saturated, stay longer in the digestive tract and might contribute to serious diseases. Eating naturally occurring fats (unsaturated) found in the nuts, seeds and grains of plants and vegetables help in tissue and cell repair and body building. When trans-fats (manufactured fats) are eaten, the body works harder to metabolize, and gets no nutritional value from them. High fat consumption, especially trans-fats, inhibits insulin penetration in the blood, and increases risk of type 2 diabetes and heart disease. The higher the incidence of fat increase, the higher the cancer risk.

Other Groups

Bulbs	Onions, garlic (these are predominantly international)
Rhizomes	Ginger, turmeric (these are predominantly international)
Herbs, teas, & spices	Mint families, uziza, utazi, lemon grass, thyme, hibiscus (zobo), parsley, oregano Pawpaw(papaya) tree leaves – dried to make brown tea or taken as green juice, is rich in vitamins, can help with malaria fever, digestion, and has many other benefits.
Grains	Corn, millet, wheat, oats, rye, rice (predominantly internationally grown)
Seeds	Egusi (pumpkin seeds), sunflower seeds, dawadawa, sesame seeds, flax seeds, alligator pepper (varieties, different names and uses in different lands and cultures)
Roots	Beet root, carrots, potatoes, yams (various colors and varieties in different lands)
Legumes	Black eye peas, lentils of all colors, garbanzo, soybeans (internationally grown)
Vegetables	Ugu, pumpkin leaves (ugboghoro), bitter leaf (olugbu), kale, cabbage, ewedu (jute leaves), moringa, kale, turmeric, cannabis, cultured vegetables, green algae, sea vegetables, and many others

Food and the Body

Nuts	Tiger nuts, bambara nuts, cashew nuts, peanuts, bitter kola, kola nuts, coconuts
Fruits	Eggplant, okra, tomatoes (both night shades can serve as dual roles), pineapples, banana, oranges, pawpaw (papaya), lemons, mango, udara (agbalumo), local apples (numerous varieties in different lands and climates)
Mushrooms:	Neither plant nor vegetables. Some are edible and delicious; some are poisonous, while a few are of high medicinal value.

Needs of the Cell

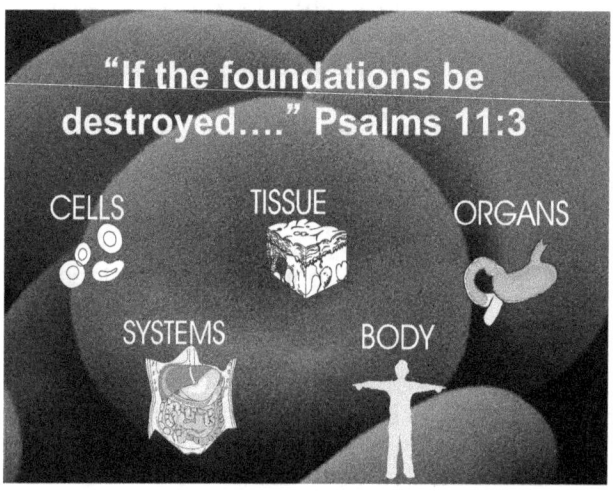

The human body is the greatest medical book ever written. The blood supplies all the needs of the cell. If the quality of blood is poor, the cells will be malnourished. Cells need five major things to live well. These are:

Oxygen – This is an element in the atmosphere that we breathe in freely to keep us alive. Oxygen transfers energy to the cells and without it, the cell dies within minutes.

Water – Body cells when deprived of water will gradually shrivel and die in a few days. The body can survive longer without food than without water.

Nutrients – Minerals, vitamins, fatty acids, proteins, carbohydrates, and enzymes are nutrients which nourish the cells.

Waste Elimination – If waste matter is not properly eliminated, such retention could lead to disease.

Freedom from poison – Retained waste (toxic waste) poisons the blood. Leviticus 17:11 informs us that *"the life of the flesh is in the blood"*. This shows the highest level of organization. To my mind, the complicated design of the human body and its intricate functions are best explained in the inspired scripture – Psalm 139:14 and amplified for greater understanding in various places in the writings of Ellen White. Here is one such explanation:

> *"The Creator of man has arranged the living machinery of our bodies. Every function is wonderfully and wisely made. And God pledged Himself to keep this human machinery in healthful action if the human agent will obey His laws and cooperate with God. Every law governing the human machinery is to be considered just as truly divine in origin, in character, and in importance as the word of God. Every careless, inattentive action, any abuse put upon the Lord's*

Food and the Body

wonderful mechanism, by disregarding His specified laws in the human habitation, is a violation of God's law. We may behold and admire the work of God in the natural world, but the human habitation is the most wonderful.[47]

Baked potatoes with veggie sour cream and steamed greens and diced raw vegetable

Blue corn chips with home-made veggie sour cream and cheese

Simple Solutions

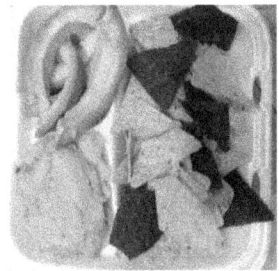

Corn chips served with veggie cheese and avocado slices

Yam boiled with its skin (skin is removed before eating); served with tomato stew and steamed vegetables

Chapter 3

Disease and Nutrition

"Those men who are prostate-cancer patients consume a diet higher in fat than those who do not have prostate cancer. When animal product consumption is compared to the rates of death, it is found that the consumption of meat and dairy products corelate very closely with the death rate."

Cancer 64 (1989) 598-604

Nutrition is the process by which the body utilizes food to sustain a quality of life. This means that the quality of any life, healthy or unhealthy, is largely dependent on the quality of nutrition it receives. Poor nutrition directly co-relates to illness. Man is a product of an intelligent design for which the designer made health laws to guide the maintenance of that design from food ingestion, digestion, absorption, to excretion. Disease results from a deviation from these rules of natural living, one of which is the careful selection and use of whole, real plant foods because they are bio-identical to the human frame, for physical nourishment.

Disease Movement

In line with the earlier definition of disease – an effort of the body to rid the system of unhealthy conditions – we see that most diseases are generally mere symptoms of poor health. Another similar definition is given by Arnold Ehrets, who wrote:

> *"Disease is a fermentation and decay-process of body-substance or of surplus and unnatural food – material which in course of time has accumulated, especially in the digestive organs, and which makes its appearance in the shape of mucus-excretion"*[48].

Quite often the condition does not exist in isolation but is caused by an abuse of a natural process. When decay sets in, stench results, and the system is poisoned. This situation progresses to other more serious conditions inside the body, leading to various forms of diagnoses like diabetes, anemia, obesity, cancer, heart attack, or even stroke, depending on the part of the body where the mucus finds lodging. The body struggles to rid itself of the strange cells, stale or clumpy blood causing inflammation, degeneration, and poor circulation. The individual comes down with a feeling of pain, weakness, dizziness, headache, indigestion or bloating, again, depending on the location of the discomfort. At this point the person needs toxic waste and poison elimination. The individual could choose to consider natural health care, which uses a variety of approaches to identify the root cause of disease. A favorite advice on approach to healing disease says,

> "In case of sickness, the cause should be ascertained. Unhealthful conditions should be changed, wrong habits corrected. Then nature is to be assisted in her effort to expel impurities and to re-establish right conditions in the system."[49]

This is a naturopathic approach – a system of wholistic care that deeply investigates the lifestyle of the individual to ascertain all aspects of the human machine to which the disease has attached.

Many individuals are highly constipated. They move around like walking, living cesspools. Dormant diseases gradually convert to active or acute diseases when the wastes are not eliminated. Quite often, diseases like the flu or common cold are not recognized as early indicators of the need for the individual to pursue a course of detoxification or internal body cleansing. Much attention is given to external cleanliness to the neglect of the most important – internal cleanliness because disease is fomented within the body. A continual neglect of internal cleanliness causes an accumulation of 'sewage,' which steadily grandfathers mushrooms of chronic conditions. Dr. Ehrets says that internal grooming is more important than the external because all disease is caused by internal impurity. He shared his personal observations as a medical doctor, as follows: relief

> "My experience from day to day developed startling discoveries in the form of worms and nests of eggs that we daily get from patients, accompanied by blood and pus. As I stood looking at the colon and reservoir of death, I expressed myself in wonder that anyone can live a week, much less for years, with such a cesspool of death and contagion always with him. The absorption of the deadly poison back into the circulation cannot help but cause all the contagious diseases…my experience during the past ten years has proven, by the rapid recovery of diseases after the colon was cleansed, that in the colon itself lies the basic cause of almost all human ailments."[50]

According to him, elimination of waste matter, especially for persons who have been suffering and weakened by sickness for a long time, is a sure way of relief.

If there is no immediate and meaningful discontinuation of the mucus forming toxic foods (which caused the ailment in the first place), the ailment multiplies in different forms. Intervention by way of personal education and practical implementation of changes in lifestyle/nutrition, following the signs and symptoms felt, will prevent the body from progressing on a downward spiral from cell to tissue to organ, until a general body debility results in disability. Dr. John Travis illustrates the concept of wellness using the illness/wellness continuum diagram as shown in Figure 8. According to his wellness model, high level wellness is holistic. It is a condition of optimal physical, emotional, intellectual, spiritual, social, and vocational wellbeing. This book presents the same concepts by addressing the vehicle to holistic health as eight (basic) natural laws of health. When these are practiced alongside the moral laws of life, optimum holistic health can be achieved.

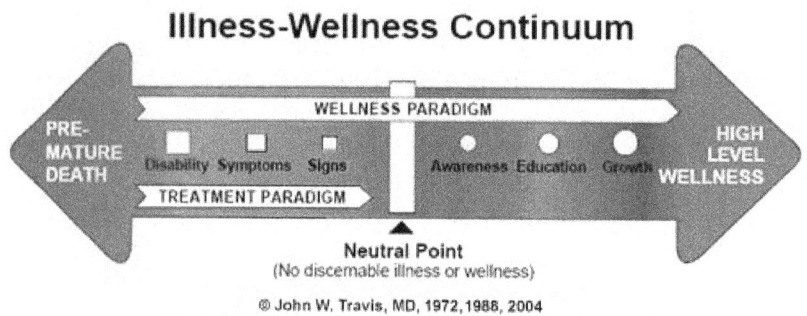

Figure 8. Illness-Wellness continuum[51]

Disease and Culture

There is growing awareness that in the United States and most Western countries, chronic diseases that cause morbidity and mortality have been found to be diet related. Whole populations and cultures are not taught the right things or ways to eat.

Cordain, Eaton, and Sebastian amplified the situation when they stated that chronic "diseases are epidemic in contemporary Westernized populations and typically afflict 50–65% of the adult population, yet they are rare or nonexistent in hunter-gatherers and other less Westernized people."[52] In this article, they also postulate that many of the diseases of western civilization have risen because of "evolutionary discordance between our ancient, genetically determined biology and the nutritional, cultural, and activity patterns in contemporary Western populations."[53]

People migrate with their culture and food habits, but over time, they adopt the new culture and also begin to experience the diseases of the adoptive culture. This is in line with the argument of Carrera-Bastos et al., that "traditional populations may have been genetically protected against the chronic degenerative diseases that occur in industrialized countries, and when they adopt a more contemporary lifestyle, their risk for chronic degenerative disease is similar or even increased compared with modern populations."[54]

According to Carrera-Bastos et al., physical activity, sleep, sunshine, and dietary requirements of mankind are genetically determined. Their ideas seem fueled by evolutionary traditions. They, like Cordain et al., opine that the human genome has undergone some fundamental evolutionary changes in diet and lifestyle from the Neolithic (stone-age period of human settlements) hunter-gatherer period to the modern age, spanning 'millions of years.' For them, a "mismatch between our ancient physiology and the western diet and lifestyle" is the root cause of contemporary diseases, which did not exist in hunter-gatherers and non-westernized populations.[55]

Disease and Nutrition

They conclude with an advocacy for a return to a mixed diet and lifestyle that will relate more closely to the Neolithic period for the purpose of preventing or reducing degenerative and chronic diseases. Such lifestyles, they propose, should include physical exercise, sleep, sunshine, (pure air), and stress-free living, in addition to a combination of plant and animal protein-based diet.[56]

Much as their recommendation to the use of the few natural remedies is commendable, I am not in agreement with the non-Biblical account of the earth's existence and finds the 'flesh meat' aspect rather conflicting with modern research as stated earlier. Secondly, the observation that increase in health span will not be achieved by any single dietary or lifestyle change without an inclusion of exercise, pure air, sleep, sunshine, and living tobacco free, among a few other lifestyle adjustments is meritorious; however, I do not subscribe to the inclusion of any animal-based protein in the diet. More current research reports go beyond this conclusion. A shift away from animal-based eating for better health span, ethical, environmental, and moral considerations is widely advocated since studies are showing that animal-based foods correlate with human health hazards. In support of this view, *The Daily Meal* reported on a debate titled, "Do not eat anything with a face."[57] In this report, Dr. Bernard's farm life at home and clinical

experience in medical school is cited. You can watch this report at the following location:
https://www.youtube.com/watch?v=OCcJq56ZMJg&t=9s

He reveals cases in which patients suffering from type II diabetes were cured simply by switching to a strictly plant-based regimen. He went on to say that other studies imply that people who consume meat have a greater risk of Alzheimer's disease and even cancer. He further mentioned that the diseases of modern civilization are not seen in people following the vegetarian diet.

The typical American diet, along with sedentary lifestyles, genetics, unwholesome food choices and other factors, is much to blame for these prevalent health harms. Epidemiological studies of westerners show that such high fat foods as are found in restaurants and public entertainment gatherings positively correlate with an elevated incidence of weight gain, heart disease, colon cancer, arthritis, diabetes, and different shades of western pattern diet related diseases. This is because the Standard American Diet (SAD) is high in saturated fats, carbonated drinks, milk shakes, fried foods, sugars, and animal protein.

In recent times, television programs and shows promoted the benefits of different diets, both Western and European, which might be high in vegetables, fruits, and grains, but also high in saturated fats. One of these is the 'Mediterranean diet.' About this, one *New York Times* article reports that "Mediterranean people have some of the worst diets in Europe, and the Greeks are the fattest: about 75% of the Greek population is overweight."[58]

In many developed countries including Japan, meat consumption has been on the increase and so are chronic diseases. The evidence is clear that a major factor causing high incidence of disease of modern civilization is not just a twist in genetics but it is environmental – unhealthful nutritional quality and lack of appetite control. One can infer then that there is no specific 'diet' fit for all but what is healthy is an eating regimen that embraces the application of the tenets of the 'natural laws of health' with the avoidance of refined fats from cooked foods and from the ingestion of animal protein. Current dietary recommendations for the prevention of diet-related chronic diseases favor gradually limiting intake of red and processed meat. Eating of mainly plant-based foods is suggested. Several studies show evidences relating meat (any flesh) intake and poor lifestyle choices and practices with chronic disease risk.

In Nigeria and other West African countries, there are commercially raised and bush-caught animals, fish, and poultry for nutrition. The countries share similar cultural foods, with respect to eating and animal husbandry. In addition to keeping livestock, the hunting and eating of animals is claimed to be a way of contributing to food security and to address the protein requirements of a growing population. It is a common phenomenon that people in less-developed economies survive or live on whatever food is available to them. These foods might include certain reptiles, squirrels, cows, camel, and horse meat. Eating habits are influenced by many factors like cultural norms, location, economic circumstances, social life, religion or religious restrictions, and lifestyle. Economic conditions affect the quality and quantity of family food consumption. West African families abroad can afford imported traditional foods. In most cases, these foods are more readily available abroad than in the homeland. They are, therefore, in addition to the typical American meals, consumed lavishly.

In a cross-sectional study of dietary patterns of elderly Nigerians, it was found that the higher the income, the higher the food budget with consumption of animal protein. They also found that about 73% of the elderly are more likely to have a high consumption of fish and meat (animal products) on a daily basis.[59] One might not be mistaken to interpret the enhanced flesh eating habits to mean that while at home, they were too poor to eat 'rich,' and being abroad, they become too rich to eat 'poor.' This is a common situation across cultures, making the prevalence of disease more abundant. According to the *Journal of the American Medical Association (JAMA)* report on burden of disease, cancer of the colon and rectum were among the 5 leading causes of death"[60].

Food Supplementation

There is a place for supplements depending on the disease and duration of use. The user must be intentional to know the source and overall make-up of the supplement being used. Whole plant foods eaten in their natural states supply micronutrients for strength and vitality. In fruits, grains, nuts, and vegetables are to be found ALL the food elements that we NEED, because the life that was in the non-stimulating foods (plants) passes into the eater. A fruit like the orange fights infections because it contains minerals, potassium, calcium, vitamins, folic acid, and much more. The pineapple fights inflammation. It has enzymes that aid in the digestion of proteins and more. Vitamins as food components were not discovered before 1912. Until then, most societies lived and obtained all they needed for sustenance from food grown from the soil without processed food and artificial supplementation. Some of these nutrients cannot be derived from artificial synthetic and expensive supplements. Taking a pill is easy but it is difficult to contain nature or a solution in a pill. However, there are nutraceutical supplements that help to balance the body when taken in line with the natural laws of health. The best of these, including essential oils, are often sold through multi-level marketing (MLM). Unfortunately, many of them are priced beyond the reach of the common man. Therefore, obtaining minerals and vitamins directly from the foods that contain them yield the best benefits because the body recognizes them better in their natural states than the unnatural, tampered concentrations found in processed forms.

The juices and oils from rightly grown whole plant foods mimic the body's natural life-sustaining fluids in ways that drugs, isolates, and extracted supplements may not. The exception might be for those nutrients found in certain rich and unique plants like the hemp. Hemp plants have cannabinoids, which interact and are received naturally by certain receptor sites in the brain/body, producing different effects, feelings, and often times, healings. For more information on hemp, watch the video at the following link: https://www.youtube.com/watch?v=cYgQNVbNXeU

Such plant foods like green juices act like liquid chlorophyll, needed by the body to keep it in balance. However, to use any supplement, one must watch out for quantity and quality. Some individuals who live on plant-based eating are obsessed with fear of not obtaining enough vitamins like B12 from their diet. For such, the question remains, where do the vegetarian animals in the wild obtain their vitamin B12? It is important to note that no supplements or vitamins can compete with or take the place of fresh vegetables and fruits because the more we depend on them, the greater the blessings they accord. Much of the health challenges today arise from improper food consumption and inordinate appetites.

The condition of the mind is equally important. If the individual eats with doubt and without absolute trust in divine power, obtaining all the benefits of the food might be hindered. In line with the words of the wise King Solomon in Proverbs 23:7, thought patterns affect the individual physically and spiritually. Disease conversion syndrome is real. People who make the flesh of dead animals a part of their diet or as a source of vitamins or proteins, whether such animals walk, swim, or fly, are making a sure inroad for disease entrance to their system. "Their bodies are full of disease," says Ellen White.[61] The bodies of persons consuming animal flesh are like an accident waiting to happen. When the right foods are eaten at the right times, God, who is the healer and who made the body, balances the systems, and restoration to an outrageous health is often the result.

The Original Diet

A search through the Bible with the intention of finding directives in the area of health, food, and dietary reform reveals more than two hundred references. However, due to the limitations of this book, only a few of these are addressed in relation to dietary change. Interestingly, the Bible, the greatest book that is primarily devoted to advancing the spiritual dimension of man, has a good number of references toward the health dimension. Only a few of these are expanded, as much as the scope of this book permits. One of the foremost passages mentioned earlier is Genesis 1:29. The Creator intended the interdependence of human life on living things, precisely vegetation without which life would hardly exist. Human beings are made from organic matter and can only be effectively and efficiently sustained by such. In every land, God has made provisions for the survival of its inhabitants through a variety of plants that grow from the earth.

In Genesis 1:29, "Every herb, seed, fruit" here refers to the seed-bearing fruits of the herbs that bear fruits. Some of the fruits from such herbs are classified as vegetables. There are also fruit-bearing trees. All the edible fruits and seeds from herbs and "fruit of a tree yielding seed" constitute the "meat" (food) given for nourishment (see Job 36:31; Psalm 136:25; Genesis 9:3). To buttress this fact, Ellen White wrote:

> *"Grains, fruits, nuts, and vegetables constitute the diet chosen for us by our Creator. These foods, prepared in as simple and natural a manner as possible, are the most healthful and nourishing. They impart a strength, a power*

of endurance, and a vigor of intellect, that are not afforded by a more complex and stimulating diet."[62]

It is best to eat your fruits first because for a healthy stomach, the digestion of fruits (ensure they are ripe) happens quickly after eating them. For challenged stomachs, it is not advisable to combine fruits and vegetables in the same meal.

Death or Life in the Kitchen

Many studies today do show that eating animal protein is linked to death. It might not be immediate but slowly and steadily it comes by decreased feelings of wellbeing. Everywhere, the quest for good health is seen as people learn the principles to improve their health. Certain common kitchen habits erode the health. These include:

- Frying foods instead of roasting, baking, steaming or boiling.
- Cooking and consuming high-fat foods like meat, eggs, cheese and the like
- Eating too little fiber or complete grains, legumes, seeds, and nuts
- Drinking very little water
- Eating between meals
- Not eating a regular breakfast
- Drinking colas or coffee

- Eating many empty calories like sugared cereals, refined foods
- Storing and drinking caffeinated beverages (soda) and the like
- Late evening eating

"It is necessary for the cook to know that a simple diet, eaten at the right time, consisting of whole/real unprocessed foods is required in order to provide the brain and the central nervous system the appropriate environment to function well. The cook cannot afford to ignore adequate nutrition of the home. Persons who eat flesh for their source of protein are eating grains and vegetables second hand; for the animal receives from these things the nutrition that produces growth. The nutrition that was in the grains and vegetables passes into the eater. It is much better to get the nutrition by eating the food that God has provided for human use[63]

"Christians are obliged to observe true health principles, not in order to be saved, but because they have been saved, and they are motivated by love to do God's expressed will for their lives. Also, a clear mind enables us to understand God's will; a strong body enables us to do it."[64]

However, one must note that salvation itself is not a matter of eating and drinking (see Rom. 14:17). Ensure that you incorporate laughter and pleasantness in daily living. Appreciate good things and people. Laughter improves vascular function and reduces tension and stress. Smiling and laughter reduces anxiety and affects the heart and bones (see Proverbs 17:22).

Change of Taste Buds

Some persons deprive themselves of the benefits of changing their overall lifestyle and turning to natural foods for fear of interference with the drugs they take. For such persons, gradual weaning from drugs can yield positive results for a sickened body. Meat stimulates its users by generating a false sense of energy. When such persons withdraw from the use of dead flesh and begin to eat plant-based, they may feel the withdrawal symptoms. When the system is cleansed from the accumulated toxins (the effect of the flesh diet) the weakness is no longer felt. The taste buds are changed, and the person develops distaste for the former diet. It takes fourteen to twenty-one days to fully change taste buds and adapt to new food substances and habits.

Affluent Malnutrition and the Protein Myth

The real victims of malnutrition are the well-to-do. These are often not inclined to use simple low-cost diets which provide sufficient nutrition for human physiological needs. Dr. Campbell in his book, *The China Study*, observed some disease disparities in rural China and the affluent communities (see Table 2).

Table 2. Disease Groupings Observed in Rural China[65]

Diseases of Affluence (Nutritional Extravagance)	Cancer (Colon, lung, breast, leukemia, childhood brain, stomach, liver), diabetes, coronary heart disease
Diseases of Poverty (Nutritional inadequacy and poor sanitation)	Pneumonia, intestinal obstruction, peptic ulcer, digestive disease, pulmonary tuberculosis, parasitic disease, rheumatic heart disease, metabolic and endocrine disease other than diabetes, diseases of pregnancy, and many others.

Campbell illustrates that the diseases in each box are interrelated and the diseases tend to be typical of the nature and dietary/lifestyle conditions in the geographical locality where they occur, meaning that they have shared causes. Many of these diseases result from high fatty food consumption. Meat, dairy, and refined/processed foods are implicated with affluent living. Dr. Campbell found that "animal protein increases the acid load in the body, making our blood and tissues more acidic."[66] Meat eating is associated with different body weaknesses and illnesses. Furthermore, Colbert says, "The fat we eat overtaxes our bodies with thick sludge-like, yellowish brown material that

Disease and Nutrition

encrusts the inside of our arteries, forms plaque, fattens our bodies, and shortens our lives."[67]

Looking at African immigrant populations here, with special reference to West Africans, it is important to mention the issue of food security (availability and mobility of food products) as it relates to the local people in the country. The eating and work culture actually put health in jeopardy.[68] Food security is a fundamental challenge in rural Nigeria and other black African countries, but not in many parts of the western world or other sociologically advanced countries that have rather wallowed in abundance. Affordability, availability, and social status significantly affect Nigerians' animal protein consumption, regardless of their geographical location. Thus, whereas the issue of 'reformed diet' might be a far-fetched idea for people still struggling with scarcity, it would rather be a matter of education, choice, and values for those comfortable with abundance. The result is that quite often persons die from lifestyle related diseases that might have resulted from improper choices in the midst of plenty – such persons are *killed by abundance*.

The most popular meat (cows and some sheep and goats) comes only from one geographic area of the country – the north. The dilemma of the animals before consumption makes their flesh doubly objectionable for food. Whereas, according to People for the Ethical Treatment of Animals (PETA),[69] farm animals in the Western world are largely shut away from the light and pure air, the situation of those in Nigeria is different. Their fate is aptly described by Ellen White:

> *"Animals are often transported long distances and subjected to great suffering in reaching a market. Taken from the green pastures and traveling for weary miles over the hot, dusty roads, or crowded into filthy cars, feverish and exhausted, often for many hours deprived of food and water, the poor creatures are driven to their death, that human beings may feast on the carcasses....Their blood has become heated...highly inflamed, and those who eat of their meat, eat poison...and meat eaters know not that they are eating diseased animals."*[70]

So, What Should We Eat?

Often times people think that a good meal must contain 'meat' or flesh food. This must be a function of lack of cooking skills using grains and legumes. A high protein diet, as well as much dependence on processed foods, over tasks the organs like the kidneys, liver, and gastrointestinal tract. Moreover, too much animal protein in the diet causes accumulation of purines in the blood and finally uric acid. When these elevate, the person is prone to risk of coronary heart disease, kidney stones, and gout, and a host of other issues might follow. For more information, watch the video, *Annette Funicello-Life with M.S.*, at the following location: https://www.youtube.com/watch?v=XGV7fyW82lM

Disease and Nutrition

The China Study, as well as many others today, highlights the importance of living on a vegetarian diet. The human body will benefit greatly from adding more fruits and deep green vegetables to the diet. Legumes are some of the most inexpensive foods anywhere, with a great variety. Grains such as natural brown rice, oats, millet, wheat, and soybeans (non-genetically modified foods); whole grain breads that have no dairy or sugar added; and Omega 3's from flax seeds should also be included. Eating a meal of predominantly beans and rice is comparable to having a meal of milk and meat, but eating a variety of foods help to balance the body's needs, strengthen the immune system, and prevent diseases like diabetes, cancer, heart disease and a host of others, The movie, *Dying to Have Known*, presents testimonies from patients, scientists, surgeons and nutritionists. You can watch it at the following location: https://www.youtube.com/watch?v=a-JMt9ASvJ4&t=1830s

The Doctor of the Kitchen

The cook and any who are responsible for the food in the home must select food to balance the acid and alkaline needs of the body, and to account for the provision of energy for metabolism, protein to build and repair the body, and vitamins and minerals to help with regulation of body processes. Healthful cooking aims at making the food attractive, palatable, and nutritious, yet inexpensive. Writing in an era when mothers cooked for their families, Ellen White makes an observation which is even truer in modern times:

> *Many a wife and mother who has not had the right education, and lacks skill in the cooking department, is daily presenting her family with ill-prepared food, which steadily is surely destroying the digestive organs, making a poor quality of blood, and frequently bringing on acute attacks of inflammatory disease, and causing premature death.*[71]

In the African tradition, the girl child is socialized to be versatile in domestic duties including childcare and cooking. However, that is fast becoming a thing of the past. In many modern families, children are raised not knowing how to cook. Such eventually become parents without the skill to impart to their own children. In a country like Nigeria, affluence engenders the engagement of paid wards (house helps) who do the domestic work while the children of the family become mere observers and recipients of domestic service. Omokhodion, in his study about the girl-child socialization pattern in Nigeria, confirms that the socialization given to children today is such that does not prepare them for domestic work. The boys are socialized to be tough, proud, independent, 'bossy,' and to be generally 'in charge.' They are trained not to show emotions and told that childcare, housework, and cooking are the exclusive work of women. They also lack the patience and gentleness required

Disease and Nutrition

for the care of children. Thus, the behavior of both the girl child and boys can be traced to their socialization.[72]

Interestingly, with regards to the importance of nutrition above other aspects of learning and domestic training, White writes:

> "Our sisters often do not know how to cook. To such I would say: I would go to the very best cook that could be found in the country, and remain there if necessary, for weeks, until I had become mistress of the art, an intelligent, skillful cook. I would pursue this course if I were forty years old. It is your duty to know how to cook, and it is your duty to teach your daughters to cook. When you are teaching them the art of cookery you are building around them a barrier that will preserve them from the folly and vice which they may otherwise be tempted to engage in. I prize my seamstress, I value my copyist; but my cook, who knows well how to prepare the food to sustain life and nourish brain, bone, and muscle, fills the most important place among the helpers in my family...We can have a variety of good, wholesome food, cooked in a healthful manner, so that it can be made palatable to all. And if you, my sisters, do not know how to cook, I advise you to learn. It is of vital importance to you to know how to cook. There are more souls lost from poor cooking than you have any idea of. It produces sickness, disease, and bad tempers; the system becomes deranged, and heavenly things cannot be discerned. There is more religion in a loaf of good bread than many of you think. There is more religion in good cooking than you have any idea of. We want you to learn what good religion is, and to carry it out in your families."[73]

This is priceless advice to those to whom the nourishment of the family is committed.

Bean Cookery

Cook beans until soft and the water is reduced. Add salt to taste and the rest of the ingredients. (Legumes are naturally tasty and might not require many ingredients). The basic requirement to make these beans palatable is salt and onions. Generally, any other ingredient is optional. Many varieties of beans are fortified with dietary fiber, vitamins, proteins, carbohydrates, and minerals. Varieties like split peas and lentils cook fast and might not require pre-soaking. The soybean (edamame) is one of the most nutritious legumes. Unfortunately, they have been bombarded with controversies and bad press, linking them with breast cancer. Studies indicate evidence contrary to this view. The China study[74] indicates that nutrients from plant-based foods decrease tumor development, while nutrients from animal-based foods increase development of tumors.

Mike Anderson says that studies point to decreased risk of cancer when consuming moderate amounts of *whole* soybeans. You can watch his video, *Eating,* at the following location:

https://youtube.com/6bgtyv3juYI

He advises that those on a plant-based diet who are biased, confused, or not at ease with soy consumption should simply eliminate soy from their diet and chose from numerous other plant foods which will supply their needs.[75] The issue is much more on the effects of genetic modification and gene mutation on the bean family than on the natural endowment of the bean itself. Dr. Neal Barnard wrote an elaborate article on the truth about soy. You can watch the video on a discussion of soy at the following location: https://www.youtube.com/watch?v=OCcJq56ZMJg&t=9s

Scientists find that soy has the highest amount of plant protein of any food, seconded by the hemp plant protein in its raw form. However, because the hemp seed's protein more closely resembles the protein found in human blood, it is much easier to digest than soy protein. Hemp seeds can be eaten whole, pressed into oil, or ground into flour for baking.[76] Its whole plant rich oil, extracts and products are being legally approved as a therapeutic option and supplement (Cannabidiol or CBD) for the treatment of various physical and neurological conditions.[77]

In recent times, there has been raging controversy about bean or legume consumption due to its natural content of lectins. (A protein compound found in beans and a few other plants). An MD, Steven Gundry, wrote against the consumption of legumes in his book, *The Plant Paradox: The Hidden Dangers in "Healthy" Foods That Cause Disease and Weight Gain*.[78] There have been many reviews and reactions to his views, as in one such review found online.[79]

There is a wide variety of colors and species of beans in every land and culture. Beans, properly prepared by soaking first before cooking, are one of the healthiest foods one could eat. Such good cooking does not harm the gut. God gave foods; nuts, grains, fruits, and vegetables, all of which work simultaneously and synergistically like an orchestra to bring harmony to the workings of the body. Legumes are so beneficial to humans that they have been used to replace animal protein as the survival food group. By eating them along with whole foods like grains, nuts, and green vegetables, positive health outcomes result; longevity is promoted, chronic conditions like auto-immune diseases, cardiovascular, diabetes, obesity, and other health woes of modern life are controlled and quite often, even reversed.

The point is we must know the science and wisdom of good cooking, including the wise use of salt to bring out the taste of food and build good blood, intelligent eating, drinking, active lifestyle, and respect for the delicate functioning of the human machinery, which is carefully fashioned by an intelligent designer. Regardless of social or economic status, people of all ages have been nourished and not harmed by legumes. Obviously, these times have seen an avalanche of persons speaking/advocating for an evidence-based nutrition revolution as a vehicle to slow, stop, and reverse disease progression so rampant in these times. One such presentation is a TED show, *Food as Medicine*. You can watch it at the following location: https://www.youtube.com/watch?v=xnKaOL2IBPY&t=356s

As cited before, the wisdom of these words still holds at all times:

> "Grains, fruits, nuts, and vegetables constitute the diet chosen for us by our Creator. These foods, prepared in as simple and natural a manner as possible, are the most healthful and nourishing. They impart a strength, a power of endurance and a vigor of intellect, that are not afforded by a more complex and stimulating diet."[80]

When this wisdom is heeded, the controversy over *'what should we eat'* ends. The importance of the effect of food on well-being should encourage every home to domesticate their children irrespective of gender, to become knowledgeable in the art and science of cooking. Meat should be substituted with wholesome inexpensive foods. Much of this depends on the cook. Some of the leading food revolutionary movies and documentaries since the beginning of the twenty-first century have included *"Fat, Sick & Nearly Dead,"*[81] *"Forks Over Knives"*[82], and a few others. In 2017, *What the Health* was made. Each of these goes one step further to decry the dangers brought to humans and the planet by the consumption of animal food. The Netflix documentary, *What the Health,* clearly opens the eyes to the realities of certain aspects of medical practice and its relationship to current health trends. You can watch it at the following location:

https://www.youtube.com/watch?v=Og62hbNl794

While living in Ikeja in Lagos, Nigeria, I passed a slaughterhouse daily en route to catch a bus to market or work. It was sad to see the haggard goats and cows being tightly packed together, wallowing in their own muddy filth, waiting their turns for their brutal slaughter. The stench was horrendous, and combined with the chicken farms in the area, the very air in the atmosphere was intolerably foul and toxic. It became clear to me that it is impossible for such unhealthy living environments to produce healthy 'meat' of any kind. The unhygienic methods of production, the cruelty, the use of hormones and antibiotics, which eventually get transmitted to the eater, make vegetarian choices more appealing and reasonable as a healthy alternative to a meat-laden diet.

So, When Should We Eat?

If you are transitioning from three to two meals per day, the three-meal sample menu in Table 3 could help. However, principle-based eating requires two solid meals per day for optimum body functioning (see Table 11). This is what this book recommends because it is in line with the human biological design.

Disease and Nutrition

Table 3. Sample Menu Suggestion for Three Meals Per Day

Day	Breakfast (7:00 am)	Lunch (12:00 pm)	Light Dinner (5:00 pm)
1	2 slices whole grain bread with almond butter; fruit smoothie	¼ cup whole grain pasta with vegetables; bean soup	Crackers and fruits
2	Fruits, nuts; granola with soymilk	Corn bread; vegetable rice; potato soup	Fruits and whole grain muffin
3	Fresh fruits; whole grain bread with vegan butter	Lentil soup; baked potatoes with veggie cheese; green salad with cucumber dressing	Fruit and crackers with raw nuts; bread or crackers; almond milk
4	Oatmeal with raisins; fruit smoothie or ordinary raw fruits (2 choices)	Broccoli and carrots (vegetable stir fry); brown rice with stew	Nuts, fruits, and crackers; vegetable salad
5	Granola with almond milk; banana	Whole wheat bun with nut butter; onions and tomatoes; mixed vegetable salad	Fruit and whole grain muffin; raw sunflower and melon seeds
6	2 slices whole grain bread with almond butter; fruit smoothie	¼ cup whole grain pasta with vegetables; bean soup	Crackers and 2 fruits of choice

| 7 | 2 cups Kellogg's complete wheat bran flakes; 1-2 slices multi-grain bread toast; apple sauce or strawberries | Avocado sandwich on 1-2 slices whole grain bread Or 1 cup cooked brown rice; vegetable broth | 1 cup cooked dried lentils; banana |

Says Ellen G. White in a letter written in 1896:

> *"The stomach must have careful attention. It must not be kept in continual operation. Give this misused and much-abused organ some peace and quiet and rest. After the stomach has done its work for one meal, do not crowd more work upon it before it has had a chance to rest and before a sufficient supply of gastric juice is provided by nature to care for more food. Five hours at least should elapse between each meal, and always bear in mind that if you would give it a trial, you would find that two meals are better than three."*[83]

Today, more study and research are proving her counsels right in tune with human physiology. It is widely believed that she was a hundred years ahead of her time. This was not human but of divine origin. Among her many potent revelations, which may be seen as radical insights, is included the following statement:

> *"I was shown that more deaths have been caused by drug taking than from all other causes combined. If there was in the land one physician in the place of thousands a vast number of premature mortalities would be prevented. Multitudes of physicians and multitudes of drugs have cursed the inhabitants of the earth and have carried thousands and tens of thousands to untimely graves. Indulging in eating too frequently, and in too large quantities, over taxes the digestive organs, and produces a*

Disease and Nutrition

> *feverish state of the system. The blood becomes impure, and then diseases of various kinds occur. A Physician is sent for, who prescribes some drug which gives present relief, but which does not cure the disease. It may change the form of disease, but the real evil is increased tenfold. Nature was doing her best to rid the system of an accumulation of impurities, and could have, had she been left to herself aided by the common blessing of Heaven, such as pure air and pure water, a speedy and safe cure would have been affected."*[84]

This graphic presentation of disease causes and effects is hardly refutable in medical practice today. With further consideration to the times of eating, since 1884, science has proved certain statements made in relation to right eating habits helpful. The importance of a good and timely breakfast and how it affects the rest of the body in the day is a matter of grave importance to the overall wellness of the individual. A video presentation titled *Science Proves Ellen White's Health Message as Truth Yet Again*, supports this science. You can watch it at this location: https://www.youtube.com/watch?v=_GH_Hl2XleA

Larry Fleming is a man I consider to be one of the most practical, successful advocates of using creative recipes to turn common, simple, affordable natural foods into uncommon delicious meals (see recipe section). By simple and strict adherence to the Bible and inspired principles of eating as mentioned in this book, Mr. Fleming has successfully helped many individuals nationally and internationally reverse outrageous diseases.

People who have eaten meals at the right time, while respecting the other laws of health/nature, and consumed the meals consistently over a two- to three-week period have consistently recorded tremendous success - healing of the body – regardless of what ails it. The Creator uses foods local to every environment to nourish the physical needs of its people as long as they can utilize creativity, wisdom, and obedience in making food choices. With respect to the use of local foods, inspiration says:

> *"The message that God has given me is that His people in foreign lands are not to depend for their supply of health foods on the importations of health foods from America. The freight and the duty make the cost of these foods so high that the poor, who are just as precious in the sight of God as the wealthy, cannot have the advantage of them."*[85]

People everywhere should learn how to judiciously prepare delicious meals from the naturally growing food crops around them. The benefits of intermittent fasting therefore includes the following:

- Better body fat metabolism and weight loss
- Improved blood pressure
- Improved blood cholesterol
- Improved blood glucose and insulin sensitivity
- Fewer sweet food cravings
- Better appetite control

- Better hormonal balance

Testimony: *In Ohio, I worked with a young nurse and mother of two young kids who had a very severe debilitating musculoskeletal disease. At the point of acquaintance with her, she could neither walk nor make a fist. She could not help herself with any activities of daily living. Her caregivers had pronounced her unfit for work or walk for a given number of months. However, she chose to embrace holistic coaching and the practice of plant-based eating, an overall lifestyle change, with trust in Divine power. This change included the two-meal-a-day plan and eating the last meal not later than 3pm daily. As a result of making the relevant changes in diet and lifestyle, she started to experience the benefits listed above. In a matter of weeks, her health bounced back. She could drive. No longer did she need a walker, neither was she using her powered wheelchair, but had an overall feeling of wellbeing. Within a few weeks after recovery, her caregivers scarcely recognized her! She got back to work.*

One Hundred Years Ahead of Her Time

Table 4 shows some of Ellen White's many "I was shown's."

Table 4. I Was Shown's

I was shown...		Science catches up
1869: Electricity in The Brain. "Whatever disturbs the circulation of the electric currents in the nervous system lessens		**1934:** "Minute electrical charges are vital to the functioning of the brain." Dr. Charles Mayo of the Mayo Clinic.

the strength of the vital powers, and the result is a deadening of the sensibilities of the mind."	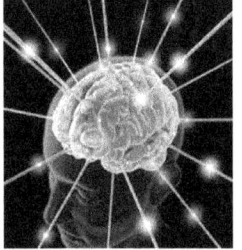	
1905: Cancer. "People are continually eating flesh that is filled with tuberculous and cancerous germs. Tuberculosis, cancer and other fatal diseases are thus communicated."	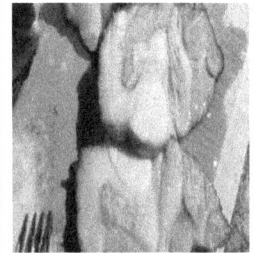	**1956:** "Many, if not all malignant tumors may be caused by viruses ("midget germs"). Thus, a large number of malignant tumors of different morphology and in different species of animals could be transmitted from one host to another by filtered extracts." Ludwick Gross, M.D., JAMA
1905: Coffee & Tea. "Tea and coffee do not nourish the system. Their effect is produced before there has been time for digestion and assimilation, and what seems to be strength is only nervous excitement. When the influence of the stimulant is gone, the unnatural force abates, and the result is a corresponding		**1967:** "Caffeinism is said to be current among intellectual workers, actresses, waitresses, nocturnal employees, and long-distance automobile drivers. Illness otherwise unexplained may be caused by excessive ingestion of xanthine alkaloids, including those in coffee, tea, cocoa, and those in some popular beverages." H. A. Riemann., JAMA.

Disease and Nutrition

degree of languor and debility."		
1864: Tobacco. "Tobacco is a poison of the most deceitful and malignant kind, having an exciting, then a paralyzing influence upon the nerves of the body. It is all the more dangerous because its effects upon the system are so slow, and at first scarcely perceivable. Multitudes have fallen victims to its poisonous influence. They have surely murdered themselves by this slow poison."		**1964:** "Warning: Smoking causes lung cancer, heart disease, emphysema and may complicate pregnancy." Surgeon General's Report.
1869: Heart Disease. "The eating of flesh meats has made a poor quality of blood and flesh. Your systems are		1961: "A vegetarian diet can prevent 90% of our thrombo-embolic diseases (clots in veins and arteries) and 90% of our coronary

Simple Solutions

in a state of inflammation, prepared to take on disease. You are liable to acute attacks of disease and to sudden death because you do not possess the strength of constitution to rally and resist disease. There will come a time when the strength and health you have flattered yourself you possessed will prove to be weakness."

occlusions." These two conditions are responsible for more deaths than all other causes combined in North America. Dr. W. A. Thomas, M. D., Writing in the JAMA.

Right on Cancer. Right on heart disease. Right on tobacco. Right on Coffee. Right on the presence of hitherto unknown electrical currents that pervade the human body (today we call the science electroencephalography). Why then is Ellen White so hated today? It's because of something else she was shown. Something she preserved in a book. A book about tyranny. Religious tyranny in America.

Rice salad with tomatoes

Steamed broccoli with onions and carrots sliced lengthwise

Chapter 4

Lifestyle and Holistic Living

"Cooking is no mean science, and it is one of the most essential in practical life. It is a science that all women should learn, and it should be taught in a way to benefit the poorer classes. To make food appetizing and at the same time simple and nourishing, requires skill; but it can be done. Cooks should know how to prepare simple food in a simple and healthful manner, and so that it will be found more palatable, as well as more wholesome, because of its simplicity."[86]

E. G. White

Eight Most Esteemed Doctors – God's Plan

God's "health system has proven to be the most powerful known to man for preventing and reversing all chronic degenerative diseases," says Dr. Jim Sharps.[87] Table 5 introduces the eight most esteemed doctors.

Table 5. Eight Most Esteemed Doctors

Doctor	Description
Godly Trust	Give your worries to the Lord. Create time for personal and congregational worship. Be grateful and keep a cheerful face and heart. Give thanks to God for the little things.
Daily Exercise	Plan time for exercise each day. Walking is less stressful and one of the safest forms of exercise. Wear clothes that will

Simple Solutions

	enable your body to move unrestricted. The upper and lower extremities deserve free movement for proper circulation of blood. The chest and abdomen should be freed from tight garments. For men, the use of suspenders serves best.
Proper Rest	Sleep at regular times daily; have your last meal at least 3 hours before going to bed. Take one day a week – God's chosmoothlys, the Sabbath - to rest; go to church, fellowship with friends, or go out in nature.
Always Temperate	Be conscious about your eating times and habits. Cautiously eliminate all substances such as alcohol, caffeine, tobacco, and drugs because they damage body cells and compromise your health. Learn to relax with family and friends
Open Air	Learn to breathe deeply, as it helps to eliminate toxins. Crack your windows open at night to introduce fresh air to help you sleep better. Do not smoke. It is important to mention proper dressing *(dress reform or transformation)* for effective respiration, blood circulation, and decency; and for the glory of God. Health should not be sacrificed on the altar of fashion. The arms and limbs must be adequately and fittingly covered at all times to avoid chilliness. * Cultivate an attitude of gratitude for the natural things God has given.

Lifestyle and Holistic Living

Sunshine	Let sunshine into your home and spend time – 10 to 20 minutes – outdoors in the sunshine daily. Sunlight helps eliminate odors and destroy disease-causing germs. If possible, have a live plant in the home to improve air quality and much more.
Lots of water	Daily, drink enough water to ensure that your urine is pale. Drink water/liquids at least 15 minutes before meals and at least an hour after meals. Ensure you bath daily for cleansing and proper circulation. Note also that a hot and cold finish enhances blood circulation.
Nutrition	Eat a large breakfast, moderate lunch (if you eat 3 meals a day) and make your supper very light-3 hours before bedtime. Eat whole food plant-based diet. Avoid all animal products, for optimal health. All dairy products are included here. Both diet and dress should conform to the original design of God for man – proper eating, protective covering.

*The principles outlined here are applicable for both adult and children, in cold and also in warm climates. Often, ladies and girls are more scantily dressed while the boys and men are more protectively, responsibly, and respectably covered. Is it any wonder why females are often feeble, complaining of one illness or the other?

Here is advice from Ellen White to a Christian mother of young children:

"Why not clothe your daughter as comfortably and as properly as you do your son? In the cold and storms of winter, his limbs and feet are clad with lined pants, drawers, woolen socks, and thick boots. This is as it should be; but your daughter is dressed in reference to fashion, not health, nor comfort. Her shoes are light and her stockings thin. True, her skirts are short, but her limbs are nearly naked, covered by only a thin flannel stocking reaching to her muslin drawers. Her limbs and feet are chilled, while her brother's are warm. His limbs are protected by from three to five thicknesses; hers by only one. Is she feebler? Then she needs the greater care. Is she indoors more and, therefore, less protected against cold and storm? Then she needs double care. But as she is dressed, there is nothing to hope for the future relative to her health but habitual cold feet, a congested brain, headache, disease of the liver and lungs, and an early grave...Her dress may be nearly long enough; but let it sit loosely and comfortably. Then clothe her limbs and feet as comfortably, as wisely, and as well, as you do those of your boy; and let her go out and enjoy exercise in the open air and live to enjoy health and happiness."[88]

Testimony: *I presented the message of lifestyle change in Connecticut a few years ago. About two weeks later, a nurse who was in the audience came and shared with me how much better she felt after putting into practice drinking before and not during meals; not snacking and commencing to drinking water at least an hour after her meal. This, having been my own personal health experience as well as that of many others, solidified my belief in the process.*

Testimony: *In New York, a colleague and I coached a retired Director of Nursing to reverse diabetes. At the time of our meeting she was slightly obese, taking more than two diabetic medications daily, she ate five times a day as recommended by her physician and was also taking drugs for high blood pressure. We drafted a two-week plan for*

Lifestyle and Holistic Living

her based on the eight natural laws of health – nutrition, exercise, water, sunshine, temperance, air, rest, and trust in divine power. She followed the recommended lifestyle change and within a few weeks, she experienced loss in weight, other significant changes, and a general sense of wellbeing. This resulted in her doctor taking her off her medications. Unfortunately, after three years of ease, she relapsed from following the principles, re-introduced some flesh in her diet, stopped exercising, and started to eat late in the evenings. The disease came back. She knew she needed to get back on the plan. As she did, God once more granted her request.

All the individuals whose testimonies of health recovery are shared in this book were able to attain better health because they learned through lectures and practiced a change of their taste buds by eating only plant-based foods; eating meals at regular times; no snacking; avoiding high caloric, fiberless, and acid producing finger foods like puff puff, chin chin, doughnuts, french fries, potato chips, and other fried foods, and stimulating beverages like coffee, carbonated, and soft drinks; doing physical exercise like simply walking daily; sleeping at the right time (by or before ten pm at night); drinking water regularly and at the right times; and ultimately trusting in divine power for the rest. They understood that highly processed sugar content foods can negatively impact blood sugar levels. The idea of a reformed diet was not designed to achieve a healing as fast as possible; the intent is for them to gain a practical knowledge of what they must do, and what they must not do, to recover health and to live healthfully. The lectures which they heard, video testimonials, and reading materials were their main reliance materials. In carrying out the same principles at home, they realized their desired health goals. According to inspired counsel, the sick must not depend on the physicians to cure them in a few weeks. Their health is their choice. From the lectures and books, it was made clear:

> *"The object of the health reform ... is not like a dose of "Painkiller" or "Instant Relief," to quiet the pains of today. No, indeed! Its great object is to teach the people how to live so as to give nature a chance to remove and resist disease."*[89]

Each one has a duty to learn how to live so that nature will have a chance to work and to cure. Most fitness coaches emphasize physical activity over diet. When diet is recommended, it could be right on what to eat, but hardly comes with directions of how, and when not to eat or drink. This might explain why persons will exercise regularly but still remain obese or overweight.

God gave mankind healing balms and natural laws for maintenance of health. Faith and prayer are important. A pastor or minister who has no knowledge of simple methods for relieving human physical suffering does a disservice to his family, congregation, and immediate community. Mamon Wilson rightly wrote:

> *"... a minister of the gospel should be equally a Medical Missionary. And if he is not a health reformer, he is calling*

Lifestyle and Holistic Living

> *on God to heal the person and he is in direct opposition to the healing process. So, what was God's plan? Call the Elders – call the Medical Missionary evangelist, because the Pastor and the Medical Missionary evangelist should go hand in hand. If that happens, that two-fold union should not be broken..."*[90]

In ancient times, the priests (pastors) were the healers of society (Luke 5:14; 17:14). The priests anointed and pronounced healing. Today, however, the healing arts have become largely secularized. It has shifted to the hospitals where the dispensers of care are trained with books lacking in the acknowledgement of God as the sole source of healing. David Stewart unreservedly described the situation:

> *"...doctors are regarded as priests, and hospitals are regarded as temples where medical miracles take place in response to the dispensing of holy waters (drugs, serums, and antibiotics, etc.) and the performance of rituals and sacrifices (surgery and radiation). Furthermore, the public is coerced into "tithing" to the health care system through insurance and tax-supported medical programs, where the amount of the tithe is not a mere 10% - but 20% of one's income and more."*[91]

God's plan is for the natural laws of living to be respected and practiced. They are as important to God as the moral laws. This is why God holds us responsible for what we do with our lives. He says in Romans 12:1-2:

> *"I beseech you therefore, brethren, by the mercies of God, that ye present your bodies a living sacrifice, holy, acceptable unto God, which is your reasonable service. And be not conformed to this world: but be ye transformed by*

the renewing of your mind, that ye may prove what is that good, and acceptable, and perfect, will of God."

To buttress the importance of both laws, White writes:

> *"God is as truly the author of physical laws as He is the author of the moral law. His law is written with his own finger upon every nerve, every muscle, every faculty, which has been entrusted to man. And every misuse of any part of our organism is a violation of that law. All should have an intelligent knowledge of the human frame that they may keep their bodies in the condition necessary to do the work of the Lord.*[92]

Therefore eating, dressing and general lifestyle should be in conformity with the original design.

The Issue of Rest

The Issue of REST is quite extensive. In love, God made our frame and commanded us to rest from our labors, just as He did after creation, not that He was fatigued but to set for us an example because He knows that after six days of labor, our bodies require a healing rest, rejuvenation, and restoration. So, in addition, He gave the Sabbath – which today we call Saturday – the seventh day of the week and not Sunday – the first day of the week. The Sabbath brings with it health and healing. It encourages those who truly observe it to relax in the love, peace, and saving health which God offers mankind. The observer basks in heavenly thoughts, and practices human works of kindness to all around him,

Lifestyle and Holistic Living

knowing that he is resting and worshiping, even as Christ did while here on earth. Mark 6:2:

> "And he came to Nazareth, where he had been brought up: and, as his custom was, he went into the synagogue on the Sabbath day, and stood up for to read."

The Sabbath is a day of receiving and giving rest to all we have and all who take command from us – man and beast. A day to cease from doing and cherish being. A day designed to keep humanity aware of the creative power of God; a day to keep away from buying and selling and from pursuing our unquenchable materialistic endeavors; a day to pause and really think about the only thing that matters most in the long run – the coming kingdom and the rest in heaven.

There is a healing and restorative power in the Sabbath to all who believe and obey because obedience (to all ten commandments) leads to health, while disobedience leads to physical and spiritual disease. Unfortunately, the fourth commandment – the Sabbath – is the most neglected of all ten. Keeping holy the Sabbath day calls for absolute trust in divine power. The power that provides us cure, care, peace, and truth (Jeremiah 36:6), still offers the same today. The observance of the Sabbath distinguished God's obedient children – natural Israel then, and still distinguishes the spiritual Israel of today and those who accept Him as Creator and King in their lives from idolaters, making them different from evolutionists. It was a sign that set Israel apart as they journeyed to the earthly Canaan, and so it is the sign that NOW sets apart God's people as they come out from the world to enter into the heavenly rest. The sign between God and ancient Israel is the same for everyone today (Ezekiel 20:12). It is a sign between God and His people; it shows they honor His law.

> *"It distinguishes between his loyal subjects and transgressors…He who from the heart obeys the fourth commandment will obey the whole law. He is sanctified through obedience."*[93]

Above all, keeping the Sabbath is not just a practice that ends here on earth for only a particular people, but for all mankind. The Sabbath was instituted at creation and had continued to exist before the Jewish nation was called into existence. The Jewish nation was an instrument in God's hand to demonstrate and disseminate the worship of God on His holy day throughout all the earth. However, the fact that they failed to fulfill this command to take the news of salvation through Jesus Christ to all nations did not and does not negate the validity of the eternal truth they were enjoined to proclaim. God chose a few from among them and other agencies to continue His mission (Acts 13:46). The Sabbath carries with it a blessing as one ceases from labor (Isaiah 56:2).

Unfortunately, lands/nations that were once Sabbath-keeping Christian lands/nations in Africa, India, and Asia fell to Islam in the wake of the Crusades, long after the death of the first apostles, and following the rise of the Papacy. These now constitute much of the Arab world.

The Bible reminds us that the Sabbath will be kept in heaven according to (Isaiah 66:22-24). God is no respecter of persons (Romans 2:11), so here on planet earth, while there is still the breath of life in the nostrils of each individual, now is the time to practice this act of righteousness – REST – in preparation for the heavenly. On the sixth day of labor – Friday – you are at the end of your preparation for the Sabbath. The Sabbath keeps you from being a workaholic and saves you from human restlessness. How we prepare for and keep the weekly Sabbath in the here and now mirrors how we prepare for the second coming of Christ. Just as the weekly cycle culminates in the commencement of the Sabbath (a time of rest), so also will this world's existence culminate in the second coming of Jesus Christ, being the commencement of the heavenly rest (Hebrews 4:9-10) – the last day for man on planet earth. It will be the crowning act in the drama of history – the Rest of *His Story*!

Uncommon Remedies for Common Illnesses

Colds

1 large onion
2 garlic bulbs
1 finger of ginger
A pinch of cayenne pepper
1 tbsp natural honey
In one quart of water, boil all herbs in the pot or blend together first before boiling. Strain and add honey to taste. Drink about 2 oz hourly for 4-5 hours until conditions improve.

Hemorrhoids

1 white potato stick
Peel and cut potato like fries
Slide into rectum (lying sideways) and leave overnight. Do repeatedly until situation improves.
This is expected to pull out the inflammation – enough to enable relief from pain. Then, the individual must purify his diet in accordance with God's plan so that the laws of health can affect healing.

Drawing Poultice

2 medium potatoes
2 medium onions
Blend both. Spread on a gauze (form a poultice) and place firmly on the infected/swollen area. Use plastic wrap to secure in place. Leave for at least 8 hours or overnight. This poultice has the potential to draw up toxin from the body. God healed King Hezekiah of Israel with a poultice made from figs (see Figure 9).

Lifestyle and Holistic Living

Hezekiah

"When the Lord told Hezekiah that he would spare his life for fifteen years, and as a sign that He would fulfill His promise, caused the sun to go back ten degrees, why did He not put His direct, restoring power upon the king? *He told him to apply a bunch of figs to His sore, and that natural remedy, blessed by God, healed him. The God of nature directs human agent to use natural remedies now.*" (2SM 286.4)

Figure 9. Hezekiah's healing

Quick Headache Help

(Cough/cold syrup – Remove phlegm)
½ cup   Onion/Garlic or a mixture of both
¼ tsp   Cayenne pepper
½ tsp   Peppermint oil
½ cup   Fructose
½ cup   Lemon juice
½ cup   Honey

Mix all together thoroughly and let sit in a warm place for a while. This mixture gets stronger as it ages. For a child, reduce cayenne quantity. Take a little quantity at a time. If available, additional 2 drops each of Ocotea and Orange Essential oils even makes it stronger.

Cough Alternative

1 large bulb onion
1 jar (bottle) with a lid
1 cup organic honey

Slice onion and place in layers inside the jar. Add a cup of natural honey and leave on kitchen counter overnight. Drink a spoon full of the liquid syrup that forms at least 3 times a day. This syrup is child friendly.

Pain/Inflammation

(Hot balm)
2 tbsp ginger powder
2 tsp turmeric powder
4 tbsp cayenne pepper powder
1 tsp peppermint oil
1 tsp wintergreen oil
1 tbsp DMSO
½ cup Vaseline
Mix all ingredients together until smooth. Store in a container. Apply to area as needed.

Pain Poultice

½ cup charcoal
½ cup ground flax seed
1 tbsp castor oil (optional)
Mix all together with warm water. Spread a thin layer of the poultice mixture on a clean piece of cloth or paper towel. Apply to the affected area of the skin. You may secure it with plastic wrap or towel. Allow to stay for 6 to 8 hours.

Meatless Recipes

Non-Dairy Butter

Ingredients:
1 cup sunflower oil
1 cup coconut oil
1 tbsp salt (or less)
3 tbsp onion powder
¼ tsp turmeric
1 cup or more ice cubes (added after blending)
Directions: Blend all together smoothly **without** the ice. Then add the ice. This hardens the mixture. Scoop out, refrigerate.

Courtesy of Larry Fleming

Lifestyle and Holistic Living

Sautéed Vegetables

Ingredients:
Broccoli
Celery
Carrots
Squash, sweet bell pepper, zucchini
Garlic powder
Salt
Coconut oil (optional)
Cubed tofu (salted and baked)

Directions: Cut ingredients into thin slices as desired; Cut onions in rings and sauté in teaspoon oil and little water until tender. Add the vegetables and steam all together and season with garlic powder and salt to taste. Add the tofu and mix thoroughly.

Serve with brown rice and sprinkle the roasted ground sesame seed and slivered almonds over. You may also add some parsley.

Scrambled Tofu

Ingredients:
½ cup chopped onion, 2T water, 1 T vegetable oil
2 blocks mashed Tofu,
Onion and garlic powder, chopped parsley or cilantro, salt to taste.

Easier suggestions:
Sauté the onions, garlic and seasonings, add tofu and vegetables and salt. Heat until all flavors blend well. Taste for salt. Use as sandwich filler or serve with yams, rice or other grains. Could top with tomato slices. For variety, add a cup of spinach.

Simple Solutions

Simple Scrambled Tofu (healthier alternative to scrambled eggs)

Ingredients:
2 blocks Tofu
2 tsp turmeric powder
1 medium onion
1 tsp salt (to taste)
1 tbsp oil (olive, sunflower, soybean)
2 tbsp onion powder
1tbsp garlic powder

Directions: Mash the above together, cook in a frying pan; add onion, garlic power, and veggie burger pieces. Cook for about 10 minutes until it's ready to serve. The burger in it gives a very inviting look and a great meaty taste.

Courtesy of Larry Fleming

Oat Pecan Burgers

Ingredients:
4 cups water
(Salt – to taste)
½ cup soy sauce (organic one preferred)
1/3 cup coconut oil (*I used no oil – the nuts have oil) and for persons who are nut-intolerant, we use only the seeds*
1 cup chopped pecans or walnuts
¼ cup yeast flakes
2 tsp garlic powder
1 tbsp sweet basil
2 tsp onion powder
1 tsp chicken style seasoning
1 tsp ground coriander
1 tsp sage
4 cups rolled oats (and quick oats combined for stickiness)
Fresh cilantro for flavor

Directions: Put all seasonings and liquid together and bring to boil. Switch off heat. Add the oats and fresh cilantro and mix until firm consistency. Leave to cool. Scoop into a peanut jar, cover, flatten and put in trays to bake at 350° for 20 minutes on each side. This makes it firm and it gets firmer as it cools. Refrigerate or freeze for later use. Sometimes I add turmeric power. Use with rice or best as sandwich burgers with onion, lettuce, tomatoes and homemade cheese or other healthy spread as desired.

Courtesy of Dr. Elisa Sharps

Non-Dairy Cheese 1

Ingredients:
4 cups cooked potatoes (with skin) plus carrots (cooked)
3 tbsp onion powder
1 tbsp garlic powder
3 tbsp lemon or lime juice
1 cup water (use water from cooked potatoes/carrots
1 tbsp salt
¼ cup oil (dribble oil in from top of blender while blending)
Directions: Add basil or oregano (optional)
Mixture will begin to change color to yellow while the oil is slowly running in. Cool and refrigerate.

Courtesy of Larry Fleming

Non-Dairy Cheese 2

Ingredients:
1 cup raw cashews (in case of allergy, experiment with sunflower or pumpkin seeds)
1 cup water
½ tbsp salt
3 tbsp lemon juice
3 tbsp nutritional yeast (optional)
1 clove garlic
1 tbsp onion powder of flakes
¼ cup sundried tomatoes

Directions: Blend all together until totally creamy. Use for corn chips.

Non-Dairy Cheese 3

Ingredients
- 1 box macaroni
- 1 head of cauliflower
- 2 cups unsweetened almond milk
- 3 cloves of garlic
- 1 cup raw unsalted cashews
- ½ cup nutritional yeast (optional but great!)
- 1 cup vegetable broth (optional)
- 2 tsp cornstarch or tapioca starch(optional)
- Spices to taste – (no measurements)
  - Seasoned salt
  - Smoked paprika (optional)
  - Onion powder
  - Garlic powder
  - Turmeric (for added yellow color)
  - Red chili pepper (use bell pepper instead to avoid hotness)
  - Crushed black pepper (optional)

Directions:
1. Boil macaroni according to package instructions and set drained water aside for later use (see step 8).
2. Soak cashews in hot water for ~ 1 hour.
3. Boil cauliflower until soft. *
4. Roast garlic with peel on in the oven at 375 degrees until fragrant and soft, then remove peel (roasting is *optional*).
5. Add all ingredients (except macaroni) to a high-speed blender and blend until creamy — taste and add more spices or almond milk if needed.
6. Pour some of 'cheese sauce' into pot and add macaroni. Keep adding enough of the 'cheese sauce' until macaroni is saturated but not overly so. **

7. Cook on medium low heat for ~10 minutes.
8. Can add more cornstarch or tapioca starch to macaroni water and pour into pot to thicken or add plain macaroni water if less thickness is desired.
9. Keep tasting and add additional salt and spices if needed.
10. Optional - add fresh sage leaves as a garnish.

Tips
*Cauliflower could be roasted in the oven until lightly cooked, instead of boiled for a more smoky flavor to the mac n cheese
**This cheese sauce recipe makes a lot, so add only enough as is needed for one box of macaroni and freeze the rest in a Ziploc bag

Courtesy of Dr. Enyioma N.

Simple Sandwich Spread

Ingredients:
Banana - mashed
Avocado - mashed
Directions: Combine the two, sprinkle lightly with salt (ground flax seed –optional) and use as sandwich spread. (Add a teaspoon lemon juice – optional)
A very delicious filling.

Hannah's Root soup (Yebeh)

Ingredients:
1 cup cut cassava root (tubers)
1 cup cut sweet potatoes
1 cup cut yam tubers (African yams)
1 cup cut cocoa yam
Directions: Cook in peanut sauce (ground and roasted peanut paste, according to desired consistency)
Season with salt, pepper, onions, turmeric, garlic, mint leaf, as desired; a pinch of nutmeg (optional)

Vegetable (Okra) Soup

Ingredients:
1-2 packs frozen and freshly cut spinach
1 sweet red pepper (tatase)
1 tbsp palm oil
1 small onion
1 tsp dawadawa
1 pack frozen or fresh okra
Salt to taste
1 tbsp ground seaweed
Seasoned and baked tofu cubes (instead of soy chunks)
3 cups water (*Note the absence of Maggi cube: It is not considered profitable to health*)

Directions: Boil and season the tofu to taste. Use the stock as part of the 3 cups of water. Add the red pepper, onions. (Could be steamed without any oil). To the stock, add the bullion, (optional), add okra (*you may add mushroom if desired - Mushrooms are fungus that grow on dead and decomposing matter and so not acceptable to some individuals*). Add the vegetable and salt to taste last. Remove from heat in time to avoid overcooking the vegetable. Serve hot with garri, yam, oat, plantain, corn, rice or wheat flour.

Vegetable (Egusi) Soup

Ingredients:
2 cups water
1 tbsp palm oil
1 tsp ukpo, achi, or ofor (as desired) – *these act like binders/emulsifier in soup*
2 medium onions
3 cups cooked tomato paste (a blend of tomatoes, sweet red bell pepper (tatase) and onion)
1 cup egusi (pumpkin seeds/sunflower seeds)
2 packs of a 10 oz size frozen spinach
1 tsp dawadawa (dried and powdered or fresh)

Lifestyle and Holistic Living

1 tbsp ground seaweed (optional)
2 handfuls of any other local vegetable (ukazi, uziza)
Salt to taste
Seasoned and baked tofu cubes (instead of soy chunks)
Directions: Blend the egusi with water and one onion. Cook with the rest of the chopped onions and oil until the mixture thickens; add the tomato paste, the rest of the water, (depending on how thick you want the soup to be) ukpo or other emulsifier, dawadawa, tofu, and cook for 5 or more minutes until soup harmonizes. Add salt to taste, the local vegetables (if using any), and the spinach last. Remove in time to allow the spinach to retain its greenness. Serve hot with garri, yam/plantain/potato/wheat/oat flour.
NOTE: *Dawadawa is a rich and very healthy legume.*

Oatmeal (Breakfast)

Ingredients:
2-3 cups water or nut-milk (depending on consistency desired)
1 cup regular or old-fashioned oats
Pinch of salt
Dried fruits – raisins, dates, as desired (*small pineapple chunks - optional*)
Directions: Bring the liquid to boil; add the fruits and oats. Boil and stir regularly to avoid burning for about 5 minutes, depending on if you like it – thick or of a soft consistency.
Remove from stove and serve with banana, any berries, more nuts like walnuts, and more nut-milk beverage, as desired.

Marian's Peanut/Soy Burger

Ingredients:
2 cups ground raw peanut
½ cup breadcrumbs

½ tsp garlic powder
2 cups soy flour
1 tsp salt
½ tsp basil
½ tsp thyme
1½ cups water
Directions: Mix well. Put on cooking sheet. Bake for 30 - 35 minutes at 350°F (180°C). Cut into squares.[94]

Simple Burger

Ingredients:
8 cups oats
8 cups water
2 medium onions (blend with some of the water)
4 tbsp onion powder
2 tbsp garlic powder
2 tbsp salt
2 tsp sage (gives meat flavor – optional)
Directions: Bring water to boil, add seasonings, blended onions. Mix oats very thoroughly. Take off fire to cool. Scoop out, flatten into circles. Bake at 350° F till brownish – turn other side.
Courtesy of Larry Fleming

Black Bean Burger

Ingredients:
1 can black beans (drained)
½ cup rolled oats
½ cup frozen corn
½ tsp turmeric powder
½ tsp salt (to taste)
3 garlic cloves (shopped)
½ purple or other onion (chopped)
1 tbsp fresh chopped cilantro
1 tsp ground cumin

¼ cup breadcrumbs

Directions: Blend garlic and onions together, then scoop out into a bowl. Blend the rest of the ingredients (use pulse button). Mix all together in the bowl and shape into balls, flatten to a round form. Heat in a skillet, one side at a time, for about 6-7 minutes. Serve with burger buns. Layer with slices of tomatoes, lettuce, veggie cheese sauce, onion rings. Slices of avocados may also be added (optional).

Nigerian Brown Beans

Ingredients:
4 cups brown beans or black eye peas (soak overnight or at least for four hours. Rinse off before cooking. This process ensures easier digestion)
6 cups water (or less if beans are soaked already)
I large onion
1 tbsp red palm oil or olive oil (optional)
Red bell peppers could be used for enhancement of color and improved taste)
1 tsp garlic powder
1 tsp ginger powder
1 tbsp salt
Any other herb or fresh vegetable as desired.
(Note the absence of cayenne pepper. It's best used medicinally instead of for dietary purposes.)

Ekele's Granola

Granola is a rich and very filling cereal. It can be used to interchange oatmeal for a hearty breakfast, eaten with nut or seed-milk, fresh fruit like banana, strawberry, avocado pear, pawpaw (papaya), or blueberries. There are various versions but two will be presented here:

Ingredients:
8 cups rolled oats

2 cups quick oats
2 cups un-sweetened desiccated coconut flakes
Blend the following until creamy:
1 cup raw sunflower seeds
1 cup water
1 cup honey/maple syrup/Sorgo/Sucanat (a natural cane sugar that retains its molasses content)
I cup apple juice (if available) or apple sauce
3 tsp pure vanilla essence
1 tsp salt

Directions: Combine the dry ingredients in a different bowl and pour the blended liquid over them. Mix thoroughly with your hands. Spread evenly on a nonstick shallow baking sheet. Bake at low heat (180°F) for about 6-8 hours, stirring occasionally until golden brown. Baking for 3-5 hours in a dehydrator at about (115°F) works as well. For a shorter period, bake at 250-275° for 1-2 hours till golden brown and crunchy. For a richer nuttier version, once out of the oven, add all or some of the following according to taste, if available:

2 cups   raisins
1 cup   raw sunflower seeds
1 cup   raw pumpkin seeds
1 cup   broken raw cashews
½ cup   broken raw walnuts
½ cup   broken raw almonds

Mix all evenly. Allow to cool and store in an air-tight container.

Dale's Granola

Ingredients:
16 cups whole rolled oats
1 cup water
1 cup applesauce
½ cup honey, agave, or Sorgo syrup

Directions: Mix the above. Bake at 200°F overnight (8hours)

Lifestyle and Holistic Living

Add:
1 cup pumpkin seeds
1 cup sunflower seeds
1 cup raisins
1 cup whole raw almonds
Mix. Allow to cool for about 3 hours. Store in air-tight container.[95]

Cooked and Seasoned Greens

Ingredients:
2 tbsp olive oil (optional)
1 tbsp grated ginger
1 tbsp crushed garlic
1 large onion
4 cups chopped tomatoes
½ tsp each of thyme, basil, rosemary
1 cup chopped bell pepper (may use yellow, red or green or a combination)
4 cups spinach – frozen, thawed and drained (other greens like turnips, collards, or a combination)
Directions: Sauté onions with little water (which is healthier) or oil, if desired.
Add tomatoes and spices. Cook for about 15-20 minutes. Add greens and pepper. Cook for another 5 minutes. Vegetables should not lose their color from overcooking.

Wheat Meat Entree

Ingredients:
1 cup walnuts
1 tsp onion powder
¼ cup rolled oats
½ tsp garlic powder
½ cup yeast flakes
1¾ cup warm water
1 tsp salt

2½ cup gluten flour *(1 tbsp Tiger nut flour might be added as a good preservative)*
Directions:
1. Blend first seven ingredients on high, till creamy, about 30 seconds.
2. Place blended mixture into mixing bowl. Use a dough hook (if you have one) or use your hands to fold in all flour. Mix until very smooth, several minutes until it forms a rubber-like ball. Remove dough.
3. Cut into desired sizes depending on entrée being used. Do not stack pieces while cutting as they will stick together.
4. Bring broth to a boil in covered pot (see broth recipe). Drop pieces into boiling broth. Lightly boil 1-2 hours. Cook until soft throughout. Yields 2 quarts gluten pieces.

Broth: Used in step 4 of Wheat Meat recipe.

Ingredients:
10 cups water
1/3 cup soy sauce (unfermented)
1¼ tsp salt
Directions: Combine all ingredients in a large pot. Cover and bring to a boil. Yields 11 to 12 cups.

Adapted from Healthy Cuisine – A 3ABN cooking sampler.

Waffle Batter

Ingredients:
2 cups oat
2 cups water
1 tsp salt
¼ cup oil
1tbsp honey/molasses/Sorgo
1tbsp corn flour or buckwheat (optional)
Directions: Blend to smooth consistency
Courtesy of Larry Fleming

Energizing Oatmeal Drink

Ingredients:
1½ cups soy/almond/rice or other nut milk
1 cup raw oatmeal
1 tbsp natural sugar or honey (optional)
2 tbsp pecan/walnuts/cashew (either one)
½ tsp vanilla/cinnamon (optional)
Directions: Blend all together and serve. Could add ice cubes if desired; cold or chill in refrigerator.

Apple/Berry Drink

Ingredients:
4 red apples
4 oz blackberries
4 oz cranberries
7 oz blue berries
7 oz raspberries
A little water
Directions: Clean and prepare the fruits, cut apples in small wedges. Juice all the together. Serve chilled as desired.

Almond or Cashew Beverage (Milk)

Ingredients:
1/2 cup raw cashews or almonds
1/8 tsp salt
1 cup water
2 tbsp honey
Directions: In a blender, grind all ingredients smoothly until creamy. Add additional 2 cups water. Blend well and refrigerate. Shake before serving.

Salad Dressing (Cucumber)

Ingredients:
¼ tsp onion
¼ tsp salt
½ cup raw cashews
½ cup diced cucumber
1 tbsp fresh lemon juice (depending on taste outcome desired)
1 tbsp honey
¼ tsp garlic
Directions: Blend to a very smooth and creamy consistency. Store in the refrigerator.

Soy Base

Soy Base is a great addition for soymilk, soy mayonnaise, soy margarine, soy and cashew milk combined).

Ingredients:
2 cups water
1 cup soy flour
Directions: Blend mixture together and steam in a double boiler for two hours (leaving the pot partially covered). Depending on the type of pot, could also cook in less amount of time. The mixture hardens like cake when done. Store in the fridge.

Soy Mayo

Ingredients:
½ cup water
1 cup soy base
½ tsp salt
½ tsp garlic powder
2½ tsp onion powder
2 tbsp lemon juice
1/3 cup oil

Lifestyle and Holistic Living

Directions: Blend all mayo ingredients together except the oil. When well blended, start stirring in the oil until mixture thickens. Add more oil if a thicker consistency is desired. Store in the fridge. Use for recipes that call for mayonnaise.

Minerva's Delightful Summer Lemonade (*without added sugar*)

Equipment needed: Juicer

Ingredients:
1 large apple
1 large pear
1/2 to 1 peeled lemon (to taste)
Directions: Juice an apple, a pear and 1/2 lemon. For a tartier taste, juice more lemon. Serve on ice and enjoy.

Okezie's Special Bread

Machine mix loaf

Ingredients:
3 cups flour
1 tsp salt
1/2 cup sugar (brown/cane) or as substitute: 1/2 cup raisins and two tablespoons of honey (preferable)
1 packet rapid rise yeast
2 tbsp olive or coconut oil
1 or 1¼ cup room temp water
1/4 - 1/2 cup raw sunflower seeds
1 tsp turmeric
1/2 tsp black pepper (ground - optional)
1/4 - 1/2 cup hemp hearts
Directions: Mix, shape into a baking pan and bake for about 45 mins.

Ihuoma's Special Coffee Alternative

Chicory-dandy coffee alternative
If you love the taste of coffee but are leery of caffeine, this just might be the drink for you. Served hot or cold, with non-dairy milk and a sweetener, or plain 'black,' you will be pleasantly surprised by the rich, flavorful taste of this coffee alternative. Not only does it skip the caffeine, but it is chock-full of several health benefits your body will love! Here are just a few:

Chicory root is a good source of fiber and especially high in inulin, a prebiotic fiber which promotes the growth of healthy bacteria. Chicory root also contains plant polyphenols, which help fight inflammation and protect the liver, and can help with blood glucose regulation. Ground roasted chicory root has the added benefit of looking and tasting quite similar to coffee!

Dandelion is often considered a nuisance on well-manicured lawns, but it is, from root to tip, a powerhouse plant. Roasted dandelion root contains important vitamins and minerals such as magnesium, iron, zinc, vitamin C, and many others. Like chicory root, it helps improve digestion and regulate blood sugar. It has also been used to treat adverse skin conditions.

Licorice root can be used as a low-calorie sweetener and contains several B vitamins and has been used successfully to treat upper respiratory infections. It also helps relieve menstrual cramps and hormonal imbalances and has been used to treat low blood pressure. That said, licorice root can be dangerous to ingest if you have high blood pressure. Please avoid this herb if this is your condition!

This recipe makes two cups (540 ml) of tea/coffee alternative.

Ingredients:
1 tbsp ground organic roasted chicory root
½ tsp organic roasted dandelion root
½ tsp organic licorice root (skip this ingredient if you have high blood pressure)
1 teabag or tea strainer (optional)
1 large teacup or glass jug
2 cups of boiling hot water
¼ cup (more or less as you choose) of non-diary milk. I used almond milk.
Sweetener of choice

Directions: Place the teabag or tea strainer in the teacup or jug. Pour the chicory root, dandelion root, and licorice root into the teabag or tea strainer. Pour in the hot water just as soon as it has boiled and let it steep for five to ten minutes. If you do not have a teabag or strainer, pour out and strain using a fine mesh sieve. Stir in your non-dairy milk and add a sweetener as desired. I usually omit the sweetener since licorice root is mildly sweet. However, this is a bit on the bitter side (think black coffee) so you may want more sweetness. Enjoy hot, or place in refrigerator to chill.

Moin

In Nigerian food culture, moin moin is traditionally made with black eyed peas (beans) pea paste. It is sometimes made with the brown beans too. Either one, not much ingredients is required because legumes are naturally rich in proteins. It is often used to accompany rice, plantains and grain dishes. This particular moin moin recipe is made in same way but using the garbanzo (chickpeas) beans instead. Garbanzo is a highly nutritious bean and to make it in the form of moin moin further enhances its taste:

Ingredients:
3 cups or 700 grams garbanzo beans (soaked and soft)

3 red bell peppers (tatase) (for sweetness and for color)
2 large onions
½ tsp ground nutmeg (optional)
¼ cup olive/vegetable oil
Salt to taste
Water to blend into a thick but dropping paste.
Directions: In a good blender, blend the soaked beans, adding some of the onions and bell pepper until becoming a soft paste. Test the smoothness of the paste with your fingers to ensure smoothness. You might use a clean commercial heavy-duty mill if you live in an area where those operate. Pour out the paste and add the rest of the ingredients (include a handful or more finely chopped onions). Scoop into small steaming cups. Steam for about an hour until paste is firm and cooked. Serve with a fruit like banana, a grain dish like rice, and roots like yam, with stew.

Lerma's Special French Toast

Ingredients:
½ cup almond/soymilk
1 tsp ground flax seeds
1 tsp ground chia seeds
1 tbsp egg replacer
Pinch of salt to taste
4 slices of whole grain bread
Directions: Mix grain and egg replacer in milk. Mix properly and remove any lumps.
Dip each slice in the mixture. On the stove top, brown each side on the wide skillet. Serve with your favorite breakfast cereal.

Green Plantain Cookery

Green and ripe plantains are part of the popular foods eaten in West Africa. When green, the plantain has high iron content. Plantains can be cooked green or ripe as porridge with onions, oil, and vegetables added. It can be cooked with yam when ripe or popularly fried as "dodo." To avoid frying, they can be baked or steamed with some onions, a little oil and water.

Ingredients:
3 mature green plantains
1½ cups water
1 tsp oil

Directions: Peel off green skin of the plantains (though some cultures cook it with the skins). Cut in pieces and blend in a blender with one cup of water. Put the oil in the pot (non-stick pot preferable if available) just to coat the base and boil the remaining water. Add and continue to stir the blended plantain until cooked and a soft dough-like consistency is reached. Use to eat soup as one would eat eba (garri) or pounded yam.

Simple Solutions

Steamed broccoli served with veggie cheese sauce

A tray of seasoned and baked sweet and Irish potatoes

Freshly baked veggie oat burgers

Freshly blended almond milk

A tray of baked vegetable brown rice

Fresh homemade bread

Lifestyle and Holistic Living

Suggested Recovery Menu Guide

Table 6 presents a suggested recovery menu guide with options based on a plant-based diet of 2 meals per day. Table 7 presents additional meal combination options.

Table 6. Suggested Recovery Menu Guide

Day	Breakfast (7 – 8 am)	Lunch (3 pm)
1	Potato Juice on waking up. Oatmeal cooked with dates, raisins, almond milk/other nut milk, banana, apples, sprinkled with freshly ground flax seed. Whole grain bread, scrambled tofu with veggie burger pieces	Vegetable soup 15- 20 mins before crackers/bread. Ingredients: Potatoes, carrots, onions, garlic, tomatoes, asparagus, celery stalks, cauliflower, peas, cayenne pepper, fresh or frozen corn. Crackers/slice of whole grain bread.
2	Raw vegetable tossed salad with raisins, pecans, walnuts. Brown rice or other whole grain like quinoa, buck wheat, Tom-brown or millet porridge, etc. Avocado slices.	Tossed salad with cucumber, steamed broccoli and spinach. Whole grain pasta cooked with carrots, red beets, corn, and tofu cubes
3	Cooked cereal. Raw pineapple, plums, strawberries, blue berries, sweet red pepper, banana, oranges. Whole grain bread and granola with home-made butter, hummus, or Tahini.	Legumes - split peas, lentils or other beans- soup. Yam/Potatoes. Whole grain bread with hummus, Tahini, or other spread.

4	Oatmeal cooked with dates, raisins, almond milk/other nut milk, banana sprinkled with freshly ground flax seed, bread/home-made waffles.	Potassium broth from potatoes, carrots, onions, garlic, tomatoes, asparagus, celery stalks, cauliflower. Crackers/slice of whole grain bread.
5	Watermelon juice (refreshing to start the morning). Brown rice or other whole grain porridge like quinoa, buck wheat or millet, etc. (casserole). Avocado slices.	Legumes - split peas, lentils, or other bean soups. Yam/Potatoes or vegetable macaroni & cheese. Whole grain bread with hummus/Tahini or other spread.
6	Oatmeal cooked with dates, raisins, almond milk, or other nut milk, banana, apples and sprinkled with freshly ground flax seed. Bread or home-made waffles.	Tossed salad with cucumber, steamed broccoli and spinach. Whole grain pasta cooked with carrots, red beets, corn, and tofu cubes.
7	Fruit salad. Oatmeal cooked with dates, raisins, almond milk, or other nut milk, banana, apples, sprinkled with freshly ground flax seed. Whole grain bread. Yam with tomato sauce or stew.	Potassium broth from potatoes, carrots, onions, garlic, tomatoes asparagus, celery stalks, cauliflower. Crackers. Vegetable rice with beans or garbanzo bean salad.

Notes:
6 am: Daily personal devotion

9:30 - 10 am: Walk 3 times daily. Increase exercise.

Saturday 9 am: Include singing with daily personal devotion. Trust in divine power. Church worship if able.

Use tofu. Tofu is a super food. Can be scrambled with onions, garlic and other spices. Use for sandwich filling.

Lifestyle and Holistic Living

Table 7. Additional Meal Combination Options

Green Juice	Fruit Smoothie	Green Juice	Fruit Smoothie
Ginger, kale, turmeric, beet root, burdock root (if available), celery, watercress, carrots, parsley, cucumber, cabbage, other green leafies **Additional notes** Eat Olives Use healthy fats. Use lemon or lime juice freely in water, fruits and greens. Add black pepper or better dried/ground papaya (pawpaw) seeds to turmeric herbal drinks to increase absorption of cur cumin in turmeric (very optional) 7pm -8pm Special Massage with a blend of essential oils (Rain drop if possible)	Blend in 2-3 types of raw nuts (**Different nuts provide different nutrients**) to create synergy and increase the absorption of fat-soluble vitamins like the A, D, E, K. Whole grain pasta with tomato sauce **Joint poultice** (bedtime) if arthritic condition	Ginger, kale, turmeric, beet root, burdock root (if available), celery, watercress, carrots, parsley, cucumber, cabbage, other green leafies Celery **Note** Hydrotherapy (Use of water) alternating hot and cold application on inflamed or hurting parts is highly remedial	Choices from: Apples, mango, Cherries, berries, guava, Guava, pear Papaya Oranges, figs, banana, kiwi, peaches, plums/prunes, grapes, apricots, cantaloupe Blend in 1-2 types of raw nuts/seeds

Green Juice	Fruit Smoothie	Green Juice	1000 IU Vitamin D
Ginger, kale, turmeric, beet root, burdock root (if available), celery, watercress, carrots, parsley, cucumber, cabbage, Other green leafies	Blend in 2-3 types of raw nuts (**Different nuts provide different nutrients**) to create synergy and increase the absorption of fat-soluble vitamins like the A, D, E, K. Whole grain pasta with tomato sauce **Joint poultice** (bedtime) if in arthritic condition	Green Juice Ginger, kale, turmeric, beet root, burdock root (if available), celery, watercress, carrots, parsley, cucumber, cabbage *Additional notes* *Best recommendation Move from 3 to 2 meals per day*	1000 IU Vitamin D **Use Top Quality** nutraceuticals like the Cannabinoids (**CBD oil**) No snacking No refined sugar Use blackstrap molasses in herbal teas No water with meals Only sips of water between meals Take all vegetable (green) juices 15-20 minutes before meal

Nutrient Hierarchy

God has placed the nutrient value of foods in a hierarchical system. It is known that all nutrients are categorized in five groups. Eat for nutritional value; eat for color.

The following chart (adapted) represents a combination of the hierarchy of nutrients and the Health Continuum, as illustrated by Dr. Jim Sharps.[96]

Lifestyle and Holistic Living

HIGHEST QUALITY NUTRIENTS — Most important nutrients

LOWEST QUALITY NURIENTS — Least important nutrients

Group 1 Basic Nutrients	Group 2 Natural Raw Foods	Group 3 Grains & Legumes	Group 4 Flesh Foods Dairy Products	Group 5 Refined & Processed Foods
Air Water Sunlight Earth's Magnetic Field	Fruits Vegetables Nuts & Seeds	Wheat, Corn, Oats Rye, Barley, etc. Beans, Peas, etc.	Beef, Pork, Poultry Fish Milk Cheese	Processed Foods Synthetic Foods

<u>Hierarchy of Nutrients</u>   <u>Standard American Diet</u>

Produces Optimal health   Chronic to Advanced conditions

Fewest symptoms ◄——————————————► Most symptoms

wellness   illness

The basic nutrients, natural raw foods, grains and legumes (Groups 1 to 3) are foundational to sustenance of a high quality of healthful living. Minerals and other plant-synthesized nutrients from the soil get transmitted to the eater through the fruits, vegetables, nuts, and seeds eaten raw. The different colors of food give different minerals and

Simple Solutions

protein to the body. Thus, a good combination of the various life-giving foods sustains the body with firsthand nutrients. Grains and legumes require some cooking prior to consumption due to the concentration of nutrients in them. Low on the hierarchy of nutrients are flesh foods, dairy products, refined, and processed foods. (Groups 4 and 5). Whereas these are the most prized and sought-after foods by many, they unfortunately place a high stress level on the body due to being laden with fats and second-hand protein. They are highly acidic, difficult to digest, and mucus producing, thereby putting a heavy strain on the digestive system.

Images of Real Food

Freshly juiced vegetables with carrots and red beets

Nuts and seeds

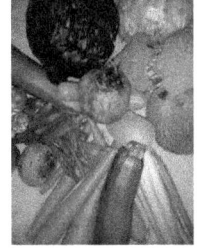

Fruits, nuts, roots, vegetables

You can watch the video, *Let Food Be Thy Medicine* at the following location:

https://www.youtube.com/watch?v=p79D6u-6pN4

For some real Nigerian foods, see the Appendix.

SAD and GLAD Diets

All along this journey, the issues about refined foods and unhealthful diet concern the Standard American Diet, also referred to as the SAD diet. The opposite diet is one that could bring happiness and healing – fondly referred to by several writers as GLAD diet – God's Life-Activating Diet. These acronyms, depicted in Table 8, tell the story.

The Standard American Diet offers more calories than fiber content. Non-fiber foods such as meat, refined cereals, visible fats (oils), sugar, milk, eggs, and alcohol are not as effective in lowering blood cholesterol as fiber foods. Since fruits and vegetables offer only 8% calories, using unrefined grains is much more useful for the body.

Table 8. SAD and GLAD Diets

Standard American Diet (SAD)	God's Life-Activating Diet (GLAD)
High protein, high fat, low fiber, low nutrients; associated with major	Low in protein, low in fat, high in fiber, high in nutrients, and is not

diseases. They do not encourage lowered cholesterol nor weight reduction. They do not also reverse heart disease.	associated with major diseases. This diet reduces the risk of chronic disease and the incidence of most other diseases like heart disease, stroke, cancer, obesity – major killer diseases.

Testimony: *In Queens New York, while I was doing some health consultations with another colleague, a man came to see his personal care doctor under whom we served as lifestyle consultants. His blood pressure had remained consistently in the 200's for weeks; he was obese and rapidly tending towards a hypertensive crisis situation. His doctor was alarmed and sent him over to my colleague and me for advice. All we recommended was a complete 'u turn' to the use of 'God's plan.' He did! Within about two weeks of implementation, he could breathe with more ease, had lost some weight, and blood pressure reduced to 180/100. He started to gradually return to robust health.*

As a health care chaplain who practices allopathic (natural health) care, my understanding and approach to patient-centered care is not just theoretical, partial, and distant, but practical, personal, and crucial. It requires total presence of mind and body, a passionate devotion of time to listen, touch, empathize, (pray, where possible) and empower the individual after *ascertaining the cause of disease.* Such an approach is pivotal to the achievement of the desired wellness. In the previous testimony, the recommendation included spiritual discipline of the appetite – a holistic lifestyle approach to personal spiritual revival and restoration of lost health.

Fiber Foods

Considering fiber, comparing whole wheat bread to white bread, 5 slices of whole wheat bread = 40 slices of white bread in fiber. Table 9 shows examples of high, moderate, and low fiber foods.

Table 9. Fiber Foods

High Fiber Foods	Moderate Fiber Foods	Less Fiber Foods
Peas, legumes, certain nuts	Cereals, whole grain flours, potatoes, yams, plantains	Fruits and vegetables (broccoli, brussels sprouts) etc. Refined cereals

Herbs and Healing

Herbs are plants with savory properties that are used in cooking or medicinally. In some cases, the leaves are used. The leafy green or flowering parts, dried or raw, are referred to as herbs, while spices are dried and produced from a wide variety of herb parts like the seeds, berries, roots, bark, and/or fruits. Most herbs and spices are used for either

Simple Solutions

culinary flavor or medicinal purposes. Nature carefully placed these bulbs, herbs, grains, nuts, vegetables, legumes, seeds, and fruits with different varieties in every land to feed and heal its people (see Exodus 30:34; Genesis 1:11; Ezekiel 47:12; Revelation 22:2). A few super herbs, spices and essential oils for health application include those listed in Table 10.

Table 10. Herbs, Spices, and Essential Oils

Name	Health Advantages	Usages	Extended Usages
Ginger: A rhizome – an underground stem. Found and used fresh or ground.	Anti-inflammatory. Reduce arthritic pain as in cases of gout and arthritis. Excellent for poultices	A great spice for vegetables, stir-fries, and creamy soups. Wash, grate, and steep for 10 minutes. May also add turmeric and any minty herb of choice. Strain and add honey to combat cold.	Available as a therapeutic essential oil.
Turmeric: A rhizome – an underground stem. Found fresh or as bright yellow powder.	Active ingredient or chemical compound is curcumin. Anti-inflammatory; halts or prevents cancer cell multiplication; anti-depressant and antioxidant	Good for spicing stews, soups, fruit smoothies. Add to hot/warm beverages like almond, soy/ other 'nut-milk' to make 'golden milk'; sweeten with natural honey and/or black strap molasses.	As an essential oil: For skin issues, cancerous growths, etc.

Lifestyle and Holistic Living

Garlic: An underground bulb. High in selenium.	Stimulates immune system; fights heart conditions; inhibits cancerous cell growth; slows down hardening of arteries'; can reduce blood pressure; remedy for bladder irritation.	Good to add to soups, broths, and teas for common cold and flu symptoms; can be added to vegetable teas. Is antibacterial, antibiotic, antifungal, and helpful in quieting any disturbances in the intestinal flora; good for enema – flushes mucus from the colon.	As an essential oil: Can be used in oil blends for lowering blood pressure and respiratory conditions. Sometimes used as a powerful antibiotic.
Onions: Underground bulb. A great kitchen essential for nearly every dish.	Contains B vitamins and more. Can inhibit blood clots; has anti-asthmatic properties; can balance cholesterol levels.	Has active ingredient, quercetin, which helps in reduction of allergies. Great whether eaten raw or cooked. Acts as expectorant and can help eliminate mucus. A key ingredient for vegetable dishes. For dietary and medicinal use.	As an essential oil: Antibacterial and antiseptic benefits
Peppermint: Leaf or bark. Has minerals like magnesium	Treats intestinal and gastric disorders; respiratory issues like colic	Great addition to hot teas for respiratory and digestive discomfort and	As an essential oil: Breathing difficulties,

and phosphorus	in children; irritable bowel syndrome (IBS); reduces stress; headaches, and more.	improved blood circulation.	allergies, dental issues.
Cilantro: Leaves: Coriander. Seeds: contain many vitamins like A, B, C, E, K; also minerals	Toxic metal cleanser. Antioxidant; promotes heart and brain health; anti-inflammatory; helps to reduce blood pressure and cholesterol levels; improves blood circulation and food digestion.	Health cooking, veggie dishes, and drinks.	Body cleansing and detoxification; antiseptic and antifungal.
Cayenne pepper: A night shade plant; red, hot spice; source of vitamins A fiery spice which is best used medicinally instead of dietarily.	Active ingredient is capsaicin. May stop a heart attack. Enhances cardiovascular performance; stimulates blood circulation; anti-inflammatory for aching joints, muscles and tissues; relieves pain; aids digestion.	Soups and stews; vegetable recipes.	Powerful tincture: prevents blood clot and can reduce migraine.

Testimony: *In a city in the state of Ohio, a young woman was diagnosed with an auto-immune condition that made her unable to work, walk, or perform any activities of daily living for herself or her young children. This was a chronic* *condition very likely induced by a prolonged habit of ingesting the SAD diet. The medications prescribed could not help her for years; her condition was rather deteriorating. Friends and family stepped in, did chores and personal care for her, including bathing and dressing her. Finally, her physicians ordered a walker first and a wheelchair later. She realized she needed more help and a more drastic approach than she was receiving. She commenced a totally plant-based GLAD approach to nutrition and a total lifestyle change. She adhered to GOD'S PLAN. The inclusion of oil – therapeutic massages, hydrotherapy, herbal poultices – and the totality of God's plan expedited the turnaround time of her pitiful condition. To the amazement of all who know her, by the end of the second month, she was able to drive her kids to school. In three and a half weeks she was able to travel long distance unattended by family. A few months later, she returned to work, and her primary care physician was impressed to take her off her drugs. Eating at regular mealtimes daily, exercising, sleeping on time, and the observation of other lifestyle practices as mentioned, helped the body to heal itself.*

Testimony: *In the same city, two gentlemen who had weight and cardiovascular problems undertook a two-*

week lifestyle change challenge. By the first week, they began to notice obvious changes in their overall body functions. At the end of the second week, they experienced telling and significant weight loss, uplifted mood, and a reduction in abdominal obesity.

The care plan cited in these testimonies was effective in the lives of these individuals because they strictly adhered to the consumption of only two meals of a high fiber content a day, making sure to balance the acidic and the alkaline types. No fiery substances, spices or condiments were administered in the food, as such would irritate the delicate and recovering linings of the stomach. They exercised regularly, had no chemicals, no vinegar, no baking soda, no baking powder, no in-between meals (snacking), no magi cubes, no fish of any type, no diary of any type, and they used water at appropriate times. An 1870 counsel of Ellen White:

> "The blood-making organs cannot convert spices, mince pies, pickles, and diseased flesh meats into good blood."[97]

The body was allowed to fast for long hours between meals – drinking only water. Such fasting induced natural body enzymes to mobilize fats, proteins, and carbohydrates while the body underwent a detoxification process. The immune system gradually continued to adjust, protect (from damage), and control organ functions like the cardiovascular, nervous system, ensuring gut activity and digestion was regulated. In this order of things, inflammation is reduced and body cells are relieved from oxidative stress, and energy begins to peak. The body chases away dysfunction, balances itself by ensuring endothelial equilibrium, as seen in the benefits of intermittent fasting mentioned earlier. Davidson opined that a reason for abstaining from eating any animal or dairy products is not just based on ethics or humane concern for animals. Someone could be vegan or vegetarian or any of the other fads and not eat a healthy diet. A diet free from the fat and blood of animals and their tissues, which often is infested with diseases germs and worms is divinely designed for the physical, emotional and spiritual sanity of man.[98]

Therapeutic Grade Essential Oils

Essential oils are contained in the sap of plants. They have been available since *day three* of creation. Why are they 'essential'? They are so called because they contain the lifeblood, intelligence, and energy specific for the plant, providing it the healing power to sustain its life and also extend such assistance to those who use them by way of supporting the immune system. They are lipid but soluble concentrates of the aromatic part of a plant's fluid, so tiny that they are capable of penetrating cell walls; the molecules pass through the outer layer of the skin, to the capillaries and into the bloodstream. Essential oils are fragrant, and distilled from shrubs, flowers, trees, leaves, roots, and even seeds. They contain oxygen molecules which help transport nutrients to the cells. Because nutritional deficiency is an oxygen deficiency, disease begins when cells lack oxygen for proper nutrient assimilation. Essential oils are medicinal and not nutritional. By providing oxygen as powerful antioxidant, antifungal, antibacterial, anti-microbial, antiseptic substances, essential oils stimulate and scavenge the immune system by creating an unfriendly environment for free radicals.

In ancient times, there were perfume makers who specialized in the art of unlocking and releasing oils from the plants (today the art of distillation is most common). These plant substances are used in aromatherapy to promote wellbeing and good health. This is why the priests in both testaments healed the sick of various diseases by anointing them with oils, as medicine. The oils were used for food, for preservation (as in Genesis 43:11; 50:2; Ezekiel 16:13; Exodus 30:25; 37:29; 30:23; John 19:39-40), and as exotic fragrances. The Bible records reference different types of oils about 264 times.

Essential oils have been shown to destroy bacteria and viruses while simultaneously restoring physiological balance to the body, and detoxifying cells and blood, depending on individual body chemistry. According to Stewart, small molecules (less than 500 amu) are aromatic and have the ability to pass through the blood-brain barrier (BBB), a phenomenon which makes them "uniquely able to address disease, not only from a physical level, but from a more basic and fundamental level – that of the emotions which are often the root cause of physical illness."[99] When diffused, they may provide air purification in many ways, including elimination of toxins from the air. They have electrical frequencies, boost atmospheric oxygen, inhibit bacterial growth, deliver oxygen molecules to cells, eliminate odors, and fill the air with a fresh aromatic scent. Essential oils promote physical, emotional, and spiritual wellbeing. They work to elevate or balance resonance or frequency of our body systems, depending on the nature – molecular structural shape (type and grade) – of the oil. Stuart says some are so powerful that they can delete or deprogram miswritten codes or garbled information in cellular memory.[100]

There are also essential oils that are purely aromatic, different from food grade or fatty oils. Food grade oils have heavier molecules and so they are not as aromatic as essential oils. The unique medicinal characteristics and therapeutic benefits of essential oils differ depending on the soil, climate, and altitude of the countries where the plants are grown.

Methods of Application

Most common methods of application of essential oils is by inhalation and topical, and some by oral ingestion, depending on the source of the oil and the nature of the ailment. Essential oils are adaptogenic – they will work to balance the body's need for which it was applied. This is because the same oil might have different effects on different people, depending on individual body chemistry, thoughts, **and feelings.** Essential oils are good to use as tools to realign, rebalance, and raise the body's energy frequency, and enable the immune system to handle stress. Their tiny molecules vibrate, and their vibrational frequency is measured in megahertz (abbreviated MHz). The MHz measure is used to describe cycling rates. High quality essential oils cycle at a rate much faster than electricity, equal to 1,000,000 cycles per second, according to the information found in the *Young Living* document at the following location:

https://studylib.net/doc/18531339/vibrational-frequency-of-essential-oils

This is why in some cases highly therapeutic grade organic essential oils work fast in seconds after application to bring relief to the user. The frequency of essential oils ranges from 52 to 580 MHz. Of all categories of food, fresh foods have the highest frequency (20 to 27 MHz). This is why they heal the body. Dried food and dried herbs share a frequency of 15 to

22, while canned and processed foods have 0 frequency. This is why less of them should be eaten. Life begets life.

Not much is needed – just a drop, depending on the size of the surface area to which it is applied, and the power of the oil 'notes' blended. You can find more information on essential oils at the following location:
https://aromawealth.com/raise-your-energy-frequency-with-essential-oils/

Oils Testimony: *One Tuesday evening, one of my daughters was escorted home from work extremely exhausted. She could not turn her neck to the left or right without turning her whole body. Her pain was so severe that emergency room visit would have been the most appropriate recommendation by any who saw her. As a nurse, she could get ready help from her hospital, but she refused to seek such help because she believed in the power of the essential oils she had learned about and experienced occasionally. She called off work for the next day. Before bed, she received a raindrop therapy (raindrop therapy will be described later). Meanwhile, she had to wear a neck collar and could not drive. By Thursday the therapy was repeated and the detoxification process caused a healing crisis that made her panic. By Saturday, she was not only well but able to drive to church, worship, and participate in* *singing. The essential oils worked and their only and greatest side effects were - healing.*

Essential Oil Use

Essential oils necessary for home emergencies include but are not limited to the following list:

Peppermint: A must have for the home first aid box. It aids with digestive issues; improves taste and smell; helps with headaches; dispels nausea, pain, fevers, motion sickness; improves memory and concentration; is anti-inflammatory, anti-parasitic, antibacterial, antiviral, antifungal, antitumoral. This oil is also very good for respiratory issues and skin and back problems.

Lavender: Sooths skin irritations; relieves burns; dispels brain fog; stops allergic reactions; and helps with anxiety, depression, and insomnia. It is anti-inflammatory, and is good for the heart and relaxation, and good for diffusing

Clove: Anti-viral, antibacterial (and more). This oil is good to have in the family cabinet. Good for dental problems.

Frankincense: Mentioned many times in the Bible. It is like the king of oils for its extremely wide variety of uses. These include balancing hormones and boosting the immune system. Studies show that it is very active in fighting cancer.

Lifestyle and Holistic Living

It is helpful and economical to enrich the medicine cabinet with home-made personal care products from a combination of essential and carrier oils, unlike synthetic chemicals and pills, many of which are prone to have dangerous and unintended side effects. The homemaker can carefully assemble materials to blend for particular needs which might be aromatic (beauty), therapeutic (health/healing), hormone balancing, and anti-aging.

Essential Drops

Lower blood sugar with the medicinal properties of essential oils like those in the following list.

Fennel: Purifies blood, relaxes nerves and muscles, acts as a laxative and has tonic effects.

Dill: A muscle relaxant with a soothing effect on intestines, nerves, respiratory system, etc.

Coriander: Relieves convulsions and spasms, aids in digestion, eliminates flatulence, purifies blood, and improves body odor, halitosis, etc.

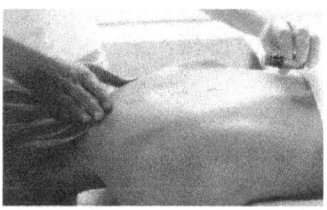

Oil Testimony: There are also special oils for healing and use in (a therapuetic technique known as "raindrop"),

developed by D. Gary Young, founder of Young Living Essential Oils. The therapy lasts beween 45 minutes to an hour. In this picture, I was giving raindrop therapy to my family member. Even when essential oils are applied to the feet through the Vita-Flex technique, it gets absorbed within twenty minutes. The oils applied on the back travel through the entire body system thus, detoxifying and bringing relaxation and balance. Before administering raindrop, the recipient's height is measured. Interestingly, the recipient often experiences a little gain in height when re-measured at the end of the session. This is due to the detoxification and mild stretching which occurs along the spine.

Raindrop Technique Demonstration (RDT)

This is a method of Vita-Flex (see Figure 10), reflexology, and massage techniques. It is used to flush out toxins, viruses, and bacteria along the spine and feet. By so doing, the technique will in most cases, detoxify, rejuvenate, energize, and restore health to the system. Raindrop releases nervous tension in the spine, thereby freeing the muscles and blood vessels along the spine to enable the spine to function more freely. If the nerves have freedom, the muscles can function more freely also; the blood vessels are less restrained and thus, deliver their loads of ingredients more freely. So, get Raindrop Therapy at your earliest convenience.

Lifestyle and Holistic Living

Our bodies are arrayed with reflex points. There are variations of the foot chart. However, it is essentially a diagram or map of the foot, showing reflex points which correspond to the organs, tissues, and systems of the body. The diagram shows where pressure should be applied using essential oils for enhanced outcomes. The technique works effectively without the use of essential oils, but when they are used, effectiveness is enhanced by bringing faster relief to the troubled area.

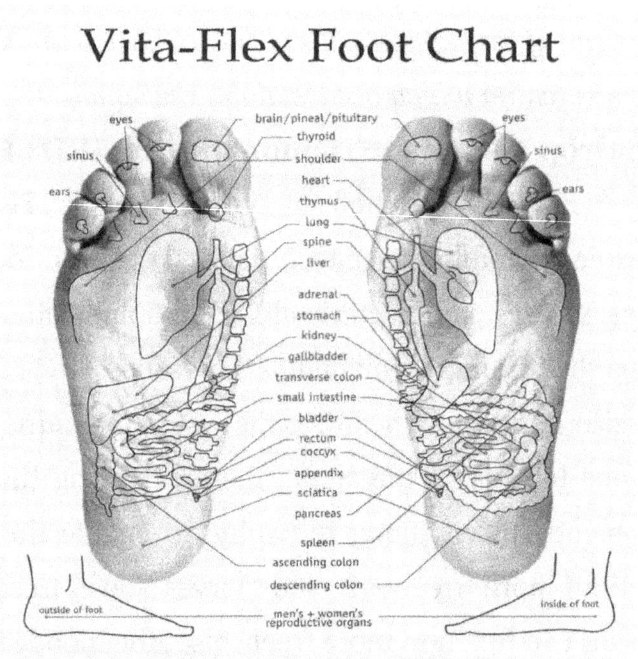

Vita-Flex Foot Chart

Figure 10. Vita-Flex foot chart
(From *I'm Oily* – Randi Cooper)

Personal Hygiene

Emphasis about good eating habits is internal care. However, this learning cannot be complete without touching on external care – having good personal hygiene habits. The practice of proper personal hygiene habits like hand washing, teeth brushing, flossing to remove plaque and leftover food which a tooth brush or (chewing stick) cannot remove; regular baths, and timely washing of dirty clothes will help to keep sickness further away by eliminating bacteria, mold/mildew, and viruses. In the generally hot climate of West Africa, people sweat much. It is not uncommon to experience persons who have repulsive body smells due to perspiration and improper body care. The use of good and inexpensive bath and body care products are extremely essential in a hot or humid climate. Simple soaps and natural deodorants go a long way to prevent body odors as well as protect the skin from infections. No one needs to inconvenience others around them by an offensive smell from clothing or bad breath (halitosis).

Deodorant. The type of deodorant used can mean a lot for good health and the protection of the lymph system. The lymph nodes are bean-shaped structures containing white blood cells which are connected by lymph vessels/fluids that travel all over the body. They form part of the immune system. Their job is to filter out substances that negatively affect the body by fighting intruders – infection and disease. They are located under the arms, in the neck, chest, groin, abdomen, and bone marrow. The work of these lymph glands can be diluted by application of toxic cosmetics on the body. As the skin is the largest organ in the body, every person should be careful about the chemical component of personal hygiene products used. Human anatomy shows that several lymph nodes are housed on the underarms. Common sense teaches that one must be careful to avoid the use of store-bought brands of deodorants, creams, soaps, and dental care products which might be harmful to the system. You can make your own deodorant.

Simple Homemade Deodorant Recipe

Ingredients:
2 tbsp coconut oil
2 tbsp baking soda
1 tbsp shea butter (optional because you can do with just the coconut oil)
1 tbsp corn starch
1 oz distilled or ordinary water (or apple cider vinegar or white grape juice)
5-10 drops of either pine, peppermint, coriander, camphor, patchouli, or other essential oils (optional)
(Some may add 1 tsp of melted bees wax for a little hardness – optional)

Directions: Melt wax and add essential oils to it. Keep separate. Cream coconut oil and shea butter (if used) together. Add the baking soda, corn starch, water (or whichever liquid used). Add the wax and oil to the entire mixture. Stir well to a smooth consistency. Store inside a tightly closed container at a cool place. Use as desired. (Mixture can be poured into a deodorant stick if available)

Oral Care. A simple natural oral care product is a non-harsh abrasive substance to help remove food remnants and stickiness from the teeth and around the mouth, which if left for a while would rot, smell, and cause disease. Epsom salt and baking soda are good to have in every kitchen or bathroom cabinet. Here is an option – simple homemade tooth paste for oral wellness without artificial sweeteners or preservatives that could cause potential harm:

Simple Homemade Toothpaste Recipe

Ingredients:
2 tbsp coconut oil
1- 2 tbsp baking soda; you can mix it with sea salt (or pink Himalayan salt)
10 drops peppermint essential oil (optional but great)
10 drops clove or cinnamon essential oil (optional but best - as a refreshener)
1 small sachet powder or 1 tbsp liquid Stevia (optional but good as a natural sweetener)
1 small glass container

Directions: Mix all together to form a smooth paste. Store in a cool place. Use a little bit at a time on your toothbrush daily.

Fingernails and Toenails. It is very fashionable these days to grow long natural or artificial fingernails and toenails. Unfortunately, such does not come without the possibility of harm. Long fingernails are associated with so-called beauty, but they are an open source of disease and other health challenges unless properly nurtured.

According to the Infectious Disease Society of America, nails longer than three millimeters above the tip of the finger are prone to harbor under them yeast and harmful bacteria. Poorer hand washing practices are implicated with growing long fingernails, making it harder for such persons to get rid of all germs hiding under the nails. It is actually safer and in line with the natural laws of life to leave the nails clean, short, and natural to avoid harm to self or others. Growing long and unnatural nails actually belongs to the animal kingdom. Good diet also affects the growth of healthy nails.

Hair Care. In a hot climate and one in which many women often cover their hair either with scarfs or artificial hair, it is very common to neglect the regular washing of the natural hair. This breeds an unhealthy scalp. The scalp needs to get air, and a good diet helps in maintaining good quality of hair. It gets greasy from the natural sebaceous glands which produce oils that moisten the hair, thus keeping it from drying out. The amount of oils produced varies from person to person; some produce more while others produce less. How often you wash your hair depends on your skin type, your hair type or texture, and the styling. Most persons, especially those with straight hair, wash almost daily, while those with curlier hair wash once a week or less. Whatever

Simple Solutions

your peculiar hair type, it is best to keep hair clean to avoid parasites, stench, and other forms of disease.

Grapes and pineapple pieces ready for blending into a drink

Chapter 5

General Guidelines for Multi-Cellular Living

"...And the fruit thereof shall be for meat, and the leaf thereof for medicine."

Ezekiel 47:21

Food is that which nourishes the body; we eat it to live.

"If nutrition were better understood, and prevention and natural treatments were more accepted in the medical community, we would not be pouring so many toxic, potentially lethal drugs into our bodies at the last stage of disease... The current system has not lived up to its promise. It is time to shift our thinking toward a broader perspective on health, one that includes a proper understanding and use of good nutrition."[101]

From the beginning of time, the Creator (God) provided bulbs, herbs, grains, nuts, vegetables, legumes, seeds, and fruits as food for man. He put minerals in the soils the world over - (science today estimates that there are 90 essential mineral elements) – necessary for adequate nutrition in the soil, and vitamins in colorful fruits and vegetables. Though the Bible does not prescribe a specific diet plan, it maintains the principle of temperance, personal discipline in eating, faithfulness, and trust in Him.

Ty Bollinger in his book, *Cancer: Step Outside the Box*, says much about sugar and sodas. He supports the notion that "Sugar, high-fructose corn syrup (HFCS), and sodas are all on the "no no" list if you want to obtain optimal health… [Sugar] is present in almost everything we eat today, including breads, sweets, sodas, oatmeal, barbeque sauce, ketchup, jelly, jam, yogurt, chocolate milk, pop tarts, and cereal, to name a few… One can of soda has almost 13 teaspoons of sugar, most of which is fructose from HFCS. Another reason to avoid carbonated sodas is that they have a pH of around 2.0, which will contribute to a highly acidic terrain. For the cancer patient, sugar is a definite "no no." If you hate your cancer, then starve it. If you regularly drink sodas, try drinking water instead. Eliminating sugar, HFCS, and sodas from your diet is one of the easiest ways to immediately improve your health."[102]

General Guidelines for Multi-Cellular Living

According to Dr. James Howenstine, in his book, *A Physician's Guide to Natural Health Products That Work,*

> *"In an interesting experiment the sugar from one soft drink was able to damage the white blood cells' ability to ingest and kill gonococcal bacteria for seven hours...Soft drinks also contain large quantities of phosphorus, which when excreted pulls calcium out of the bones. Heavy users of soft drinks will have osteoporosis along with their damaged arteries."* [103]

Guidelines for Optimal Health

Following are guidelines to follow for optimal health.

- Avoid processed sugar

  "The less sweet foods that are eaten, the better; these cause disturbances in the stomach and produce impatience and irritability in those who accustom themselves to their use." [104]

- Use unsweetened fruit juices and not heavily sugared ones.

- Avoid sweet deserts like pudding because they have milk, eggs, and sugar.

- Use carob instead of chocolate. It is important to note that drinking of any substance which contains alcohol or caffeine in any form may damage any organ or tissue from head to toe. Eating the raw fleshy, milky juice from the pod of the cocoa fruit tree (a tree indigenous to the tropical regions of the world) is delicious and harmless. However, heavy processing involving additives alter the chemical content of food, removing the naturalness. Chocolate is one beverage which has controversial press regarding the dangers and benefits of its consumption. Habitual consumers of chocolate or cocoa drinkers may experience a 'high' which might last for a short time. When there is a delayed consumption, the individual might experience some level of anxiety, irritability, less alertness, and disharmony, thus, causing a thirst for more. Though chocolate might have some benefits, continued use leads to addiction. Chocolate may contain (or actually contains as much research shows) harmful bacteria and toxic elements. Like coffee, it is addictive because of its high caffeine and sugar content. Frequent consumption over time has been known to cause unsteady balance, allergies, tiredness, insomnia, voice alteration, finger tremor, heart irregularities, and some other uncomfortable symptoms. Moreover, there is a high risk of weight gain and the cardiovascular risks which accompany such a physiological imbalance. It is therefore rather more advisable to substitute its use for more antioxidants containing natural, unrefined fruits and vegetables. As a better alternative to chocolate, carob powder from the long pods of the carob tree – a leguminous tree grown mostly in the Middle Eastern regions of the world – should be consumed. Carob powder, like other legumes, is highly nutritional and contains natural sugar, calcium, B vitamins, protein, pectin (fiber), and other trace minerals. Carob can, therefore, be used in any recipe which calls for cocoa or chocolate.

- Try and eat a good breakfast.
- Eat more fiber foods. Fruits and vegetables contain fiber.
- Do not eat between meals as this practice impacts proper digestion.
- Get adequate rest, pure water, and sunshine as much as possible.
- Make an effort to get regular/moderate exercise. Walking is very beneficial.
- Do not use alcohol or tobacco.
- Eat unrefined whole grain, unprocessed cereals, and eliminate or drastically reduce use of animal fats and protein.
- Eliminate tea and coffee. Make herbal teas naturally from fresh or dried unprocessed herbs you can trust.
- Avoid trans fats (hydrogenated vegetable oils) and foods cooked with it like doughnuts, potato chips, french fries, etc. Trans fats may preserve and improve the taste of food, but because your body struggles with breaking them down, be careful. They are

implicated in cardiac disease, high levels of cholesterol, and even cancer.

- For complete protein in the diet, individuals have to eat a combination of grains, legumes, fruits, nuts, seeds, and vegetables. These plant proteins, eaten in combination, are easier to digest, as some nutrients are better absorbed synergistically. Proteins stabilize blood sugar. Pre-soaking grains, legumes, nuts, and seeds before eating or cooking helps to improve digestion. Nuts and legumes are heart healthy.

- Inflammation is the forerunner for most diseases. There is practically one disease – the acidification of the body due to what goes into it. Refined sugars and animal protein quite often cause acidity and subsequently, breakdown in cellular communication. When the body tissues become too acidic, an imbalance is created, which sets the stage for disease. Naturally, our biological make up is from complex interconnected molecules to cells - interconnected molecules to tissues – interconnected cells to organs – interconnected tissues, which now form the entire complex, delicate structural system called LIFE. These are all held in saline fluid – water. When all parts of the system (like an orchestra) perform their assigned signaling activities harmoniously, there will not be a breakdown in cellular communication.

General Guidelines for Multi-Cellular Living

- Even if you do not drink alcohol, you might be producing it in your stomach by drinking with your meals, thus causing fermentation.
- Avoid store-bought salad dressings because of their unwholesomeness due to vinegar. The inspired writer said:

> *"The salads are prepared with oil and vinegar, fermentation takes place in the stomach, and the food does not digest, but decays or putrefies; as a consequence, the blood is not nourished, but becomes filled with impurities, and liver and kidney difficulty appear."*[105]

To lose weight, reduce blood pressure, control or reverse diabetes (blood sugar), the following how-to's are recommended:

- Eat less of or avoid completely as much as possible, bad carbohydrates (sugars). They may be in the form of pop, juice, or Kool-Aid.
- Avoid artificial sweeteners because they have been directly linked to various health problems for young and old. Kids' nutrition is a must. It is the duty of parents to guide the children in both religious and physical experiences. Busyness or the work ethic are not justified excuses for failure to teach the children pertinent issues of life. Dr. J. Terrell rightly stated that physiology should be understood and taught to "children from the earliest dawn of their reason, that

they might understand the cause of disease"[106]. "From childhood, teach every child about food," says Jamie Oliver in his 2010 food revolution TED talk, as shown in the video you can watch at this location: https://www.youtube.com/watch?v=go_QOzc79Uc&t=25s

- Additionally, teach children self-control and respect for their superiors who have experienced a sense of judgment which enables them to move from reason to principle in general living. Children must be taught that such judgment will help them even in matters of food consumption.
- Eat good carbohydrates (starches) because they have fiber. Eat beans (legumes), vegetables, oatmeal/granola, whole grain cereal like buckwheat, whole grain bread, and some fruit.
- Sprinkle ground flax seeds on food to increase fiber and to supply omega 3 essential fatty acids in the diet. About 3-5% of the omega 3's found in plants eventually gets converted to brain-building omega 3's DHA and EPA
- Avoid the bad fats like meat fat (milk, cheese and animal products), hydrogenated fats, fried foods.

"The beef industry has contributed to more American deaths than all the wars of this century, all-natural disasters, and all automobile accidents combined. If beef is your idea of "real food for real people" you'd better live real close to a real good hospital."[107]

General Guidelines for Multi-Cellular Living

- Avoid salty foods. Limit sodium intake. Be sure to use good quality salt.
- Include more good fats as found in nuts like walnuts, pecans, almonds, bambara, tiga nuts, ukwa, and coconut. Eat olive fruits, avocado pear, good quality olive and soybean oils (very sparingly), but best avoided if a fair number of raw nuts are being consumed on a regular basis.
- Eat more cruciferous vegetables like collard greens, kale, broccoli, cauliflower, steamed or raw. (Kale is a very hard vegetable and is best cooked for ease of digestion).
- Be sure to drink water. The human body is generally made up of 60-75% water, though some individual parts like the brain, heart, and lungs may have more. Thirst is the result of dehydration. At the point of feeling thirsty the individual has lost significant amount of body water (2-3%).[108] Drink at least 8 cups of water a day to keep the body hydrated. However, as mentioned earlier, do not drink with your meals.
- Walk. Go for a walk daily. Walking affects the heart, helps in stretching muscles and the overall body. Walking is the best exercise and just a 10 minutes' walk makes a difference in blood circulation, so 1 to ½ an hour's walk is good.

- Plan to eat meals at regular times each day. Eating between the hours of 7-9 am and 5 to 6 hours before the next meal is a beneficial practice. In the long run, two meals are better than three meals per day, especially for an adult person not involved in heavy physical activity. If a 3rd meal is desired, efforts should be made to ensure adequate nutrient/fiber composition.[109] It is not advisable to eat a high protein meal or snack at night. Such a practice is unnatural to human physiology and the timely rhythms by which it functions best. Mealtimes should be regular, as much as possible, while snacking (eating between meals) is best avoided.
- Praise, pray, and worship God the Creator, in private, family, and moreover, in corporate worship. When God says "Remember" it is serious. God has given humans six days to work and the seventh for rest and restoration. The 'rest' here is different from sleep. Rest is essentially taking a break to do things that restore the body and mind, something that relaxes, which brings peace and joy, something which brings good social ties, relationships, and a good support system too. In this regard, God's 'choice day,' the Sabbath day, provides such a mental, physical and spiritual rest. It is given for a delight, a special relaxation with others in a communal sense, as a

General Guidelines for Multi-Cellular Living

memorial, a sign between Him and mankind to continually affirm His creatorship of heaven and earth. It brings Sabbath blessings every week to those who become His friends and who join other believers in worship and rest, in keeping with the commandments. No other day of the week is so designed and blessed for here and in eternity. See Exodus 20:8-11; 31:17; Ezekiel 20:12; Isaiah 58:13, 14; Mark 2:27, 28; John 14: 15; 15:14; Revelation 1:10; 14:6, 7.

- Do not defraud but give God what is due Him as in Malachi 3:10. Such money, rightly used, is set apart for the sustenance of persons who work in ministry to spread the gospel – good news of salvation.
- Oftentimes the accumulation of chemical compounds in certain foods (purines) form uric acid clusters around the joints, causing arthritic or gouty pains (depending on the location). Application of ginger poultice quite often removes the toxins. Soaking the affected area in water to which a generous amount of apple cider vinegar (3-4 cups) has been added, brings relief by pulling out the uric acid. This also works for yeast or candida infections when used to soak in a bathtub. The apple cider vinegar destroys the

pathogenic bacteria. Epsom salt could also be utilized to sooth and gradually reduce inflammation.
- Food should be carefully selected for quality and not quantity because the brain and the eyes are most affected by good or poor nutrition.
- A totally plant-based diet is recommended because it helps you to avoid contracting parasites and other diseases that are borne by animals used as food. Other benefits include a reduction in developing degenerative diseases, chronic conditions like - obesity, cancer, heart disease, arthritis, diabetes, asthma, and other respiratory issues. It generally enables you to feel lighter and maintain a better quality of life. A plant-based diet helps to protect the brain. It also improves the mood. At best, meat and all its derivatives should be left alone (see Figure 11).

Dairy, animal protein (flesh foods), processed sugar, and all processed food should be avoided completely for optimum health. Plant proteins have no cholesterol, while animal proteins have. Pork tissue is infested with parasites, and for this reason, God said in Deuteronomy 14:8,

> *"And you may not eat the pig. It has split hooves but does not chew the cud, so it is ceremonially unclean for you. You may not eat the meat of these animals or even touch their carcasses."*

General Guidelines for Multi-Cellular Living

Science backs up these findings today so that none can confidently claim that such health laws were limited to the Jewish nation. Biblical health laws were already in place long before there was any 'Jew.' For better health and quality of life, natural plant substitutes are suggested instead of flesh.

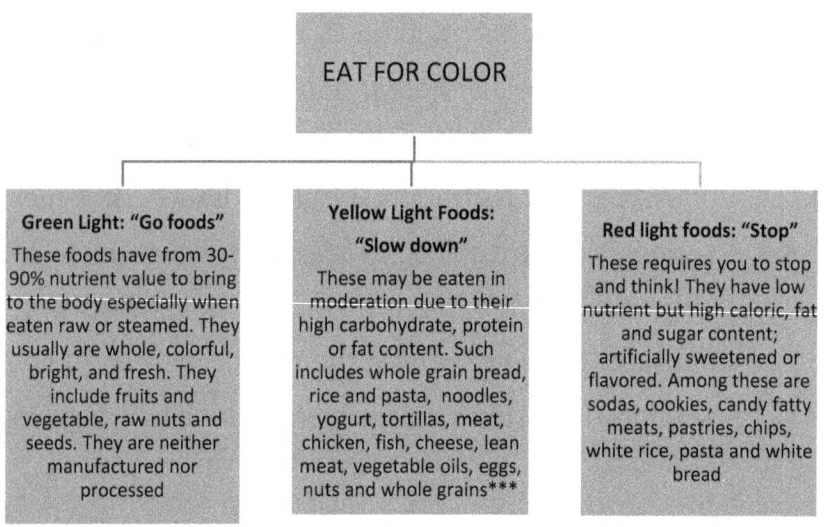

Figure 11. Eat from recommended categories of food
(as suggested by Dr. William Sears)

All-natural foods have the essential amino acids necessary for human growth, but there are proteins of higher or lower biological value. It is advocated that a variety of foods be eaten to make up for lack of others. Most persons look to meat for the supply of protein. But we can find all we need in plants. Legumes like soybeans and garbanzos are a blessing because they have high biological value. Each of these can be made into a variety of dishes that when combined with grains supply a balanced quality of amino acids in the diet.

Two-Week Meal Challenge

The world is in a period of nutrition and general lifestyle crisis and dietary confusion. Correct literacy in eating, dressing, music, and worship is of absolute necessity. Plant-based nutrition gets rid of mucus and all diseases, potentially slows down the aging process, benefits not just the physical but the emotional, and unclogs the mind. When the mind is clear, spiritual things can then be more readily discernible.

Table 3 shows a possible three-meal-a-day plan. However, two meals a day are better for optimal health. A two-meal-a-day plan is not based on calorie counting; neither is it focused on portion control. Part of the beauty, fearfulness, and uniqueness of the human body is the special fashioning of growth and digestive hormones such that they regularly perform their building and repair activities in a systematic order. One of such hormones is the somatotropin growth hormone. It stimulates cell regeneration and cell reproduction in humans and other animals. It is produced by the pituitary gland and generates growth in both adolescents and children. It works in the smooth running of all body functions. Eating only two meals per day is an easy way to encourage overall wellness. It is an eating style/choice sometimes regarded as intermittent fasting or early time-restricted feeding (eTRF) in humans. This practice requires eating a good and early breakfast and nothing else but water in-between (not during or with the meal); then eating the second and last meal for the day before or by 3pm daily. Thus, a long period of *fasting* for 17-18 hours in each 24-hour period is encouraged.

The resulting physiological benefit is often a significant loss of weight and improved general sense of wellness. Practicing this supports the natural circadian rhythm in which humans are naturally programmed to burn fuel during the day.[110] The more commonly practiced 24-hour style of eating, therefore, does not synchronize with the natural laws of caloric burning designed by our Creator. See Table 11 for a suggested two-week meal plan.

Simple Solutions

Table 11. Simple Two-Week Meal Plan
Week 1

Day	Breakfast (7 – 8:30 am)	Lunch (2 – 3 pm)
Sunday	Waffles with syrup **or** whole grain bread with butter, apple sauce **or** 2-3 types of fruit. Oatmeal sweetened with dates and raisins; almond/soymilk	Brown rice or macaroni with tomato sauce/stew; steamed vegetables and Tofu wedges
Monday	Granola with almond/soymilk with raw nuts. Banana, pineapple, and avocado pear or guacamole. Cookies	Lentil soup with spaghetti porridge, corn chips, and cheese. Carrot salad
Tuesday	Scrambled tofu with veggie burger crumbles, bread, and almond milk. Fruit smoothie	Mashed potatoes; bean porridge, tossed green salad. Pizza
Wednesday	Bulgar wheat with almond milk, fruits, raw nuts. Pancakes	Boiled Plantain/yam with tomato sauce; steamed vegetables
Thursday	Baked potatoes; cheese/ sour cream. Cooked kale or steamed spinach or green peas	*A local vegetable/spinach and egusi or okra soup with garri/fufu/wheat or oat flour **or** vegetable rice with bean soup
Friday	Oatmeal cooked with dates, raisins, almond milk, or other nut milk, banana, strawberries or pears. Sprinkle oatmeal with freshly ground flax seed. Bread or waffles	Tossed salad with cucumber, steamed broccoli, and spinach. Whole grain pasta cooked with carrots, red beets, corn, and tofu cubes

General Guidelines for Multi-Cellular Living

| Saturday/Sabbath | Raw vegetable tossed salad with raisins, pecans, walnuts. Brown rice **or** other whole grain like quinoa, buck wheat, or millet, etc. Avocado | Baked variety of potatoes with stew, raw vegetables, brown rice, and beans |

Week 2

Day	Breakfast (7 – 8:30 am)	Lunch (2 – 3 pm)
Sunday	Grape, pineapple and ginger drink. Potato variety mix. Baked. Serve with string beans/peas and stew. Cookies	Whole grain pasta with sauce; raw salad with vegetable dressing
Monday	Granola, almond/soymilk with raw nuts. 2 slices of whole grain bread, banana, pineapple, avocado pear, or guacamole	Sweet potatoes/cocoyam/or other yam variety. Steamed vegetables
Tuesday	Potassium broth (Potatoes, carrots, onions, garlic, tomatoes, asparagus, celery stalks, cauliflower) Crackers/2 slices toasted whole grain bread	Black beans with coconut and ripe plantains. Pizza
Wednesday	Scrambled tofu with veggie burger crumbles, bread, and Almond milk. Fruit smoothie	Chickpea (Garbanzo bean) salad. 2 slices of whole grain bread
Thursday	Waffles with syrup **or** whole grain bread with butter. Apple sauce **or** 2-3 types of fruit. Oatmeal sweetened with dates and raisins; almond/soymilk.	*A local vegetable/spinach and Egusi or Okra soup with Garri/Fufu/Wheat or Oat flour; **OR**: vegetable rice with bean soup

Friday	Quinoa, brown or yellow akamu/ogi (pap), millet porridge, Tom Brown Whole Grain Bread	Baked potatoes, guacamole, and raw salad vegetables
Saturday/Sabbath	Avocado pear, macaroni and cheese. Scrambled tofu, fruit medley	Lentil soup, French toast, peanut butter/honey, raw vegetables, and nuts

*Adaptable to cultural taste. However, use of hot spices, Maggi cubes or such seasonings like it must be avoided.
- ✓ Carrot or other home-made vegetable juice could be used as food with the meal, not water.
- ✓ Cheese, salad dressing, apple sauce, veggie burger, almond milk, butter, waffle, pizza, pancakes, cookies, smoothie are home made.
- ✓ Oils recommended include coconut, olive, soybean, red palm oil, and sunflower (all in moderate amounts).
- ✓ Suggested: Saturday meals - prepared the previous day, Friday, and warmed before serving.

Encouragements:

Read the Bible daily. It strengthens the intellect.

3 John 2
Beloved, I wish above all things that thou mayest prosper and be in health, even as thy soul prospereth.

1 Corinthians 10:31
Whether therefore ye eat, or drink, or whatsoever ye do, do all to the glory of God.

Run from alcohol. It damages your frontal lobe.

Proverbs 4:23
Keep thy heart with all diligence; for out of it are the issues of life.

Summary and Conclusion

In Genesis 1, the first story was one of banishment due to disobedience coupled with lack of appetite control. In

General Guidelines for Multi-Cellular Living

Daniel 1, a story of social elevation and spiritual growth due to appetite control and obedience to God was presented. What the body is fed is important to God because He wants the good of man (1 Corinthians. 6:15, 19, 20; 10:31). Eating the right things at the right time means achieving the right health. I can imagine that every individual wants to make progress with God's help, each wants to grow in knowledge of God's laws which govern our physical and, most importantly, spiritual lives. Jesus says in John 14:6, "*I am the truth*"; 17:17, "*Your word is truth,*" and the psalmist says in Psalm 119:142, "*Your law is truth.*" White writes:

> "*God is as truly the author of physical laws as He is author of the moral law. His law is written with His own finger upon every nerve, every muscle, every faculty, which has been entrusted to man...When men and women are truly converted, they will conscientiously regard the laws of life that God has established in their being, thus seeking to avoid physical, mental, and moral feebleness. Obedience to these laws must be made a matter of personal duty. We ourselves must suffer the ills of violated law. We must answer to God for our habits and practices. Therefore, the question for us is not, "What will the world say?" but, "How shall I, claiming to be a Christian, treat the habitation God has given me? Shall I work for my highest temporal and spiritual good by keeping my body as a temple for the indwelling of the Holy Spirit, or shall I sacrifice myself to the world's ideas and practices?... God has formed laws which govern our constitutions, and these laws which He has placed in our being are divine, and for every transgression there is affixed a penalty, which must sooner or later be realized. The majority of diseases which the human family have been and still are suffering under, they have created by ignorance of their own organic laws. They seem indifferent in regard to the matter of health, and work*

perseveringly to tear themselves to pieces, and when broken down and debilitated in body and mind, send for the doctor and drug themselves to death."[111]

Eating the natural or 'green light' (right) foods is like eating 'young' foods; eating the 'red light' foods is like eating 'old' (wrong) foods. The more 'young' foods in the body, the lighter and healthier the blood will be. The better the circulation, the better likelihood there is of achieving longevity. It is important to note that old age does not engender sickness, but sickness engenders rapid aging. In other words, people do not get sick because of old age, but people get old because of sickness. Regardless of drugs used or therapies or exercises performed, disease will not completely be eradicated as long as wrong habits are cherished, and the wrong foods are continually ingested, thus constantly introducing mucus and stress, which breeds disease in the system.

Natural Remedies

Real Food

Nature uses the natural remedies found in 'real food' – nuts, seeds, herbs, fruit, grains, and essential oils, – to tame the issues in human life, to pull out the physical and emotional cancers growing in the tissues. Unfortunately, due to the man-made soy and gluten controversies, these important plant proteins are made to scare instead of care for human life as divinely designed.

Digestive disorders are very likely to arise due to poor eating habits and consumption of compromised food, which in turn compromises the gut – a part of the digestive system so richly supplied with nerves that it is often referred to as the 'gut brain.' This is why food affects behavior. Soy is hard concentrated protein but when made into tofu, it becomes pre-digested and even babies can eat it. Some detest whole wheat bread because it is not easily digested, but when toasted, it becomes more digestible. Digestive issues arise because of methods of cooking, quality of food, and eating habits.

Black Strap Molasses

Use black strap molasses (organic and un-sulphured) regularly in beverages. It is a very valuable food to have in the food pantry because it contains an excellent supply of B vitamins and an array of minerals. It is the dark residue that remains as a byproduct from the last stages of the extraction of sugar from the raw sugar cane. It is an alkali-forming food, beneficial for maintaining a proper acid-alkali balance in the body. Some of the mineral benefits supplied by it includes iron, potassium, chromium, calcium, copper, zinc, manganese, magnesium, phosphoric acid, choline, and selenium.

Building Iron in the Blood

Use natural fruits to build iron in the blood in the case of anemia. This is easily done by mixing 1 cup each of figs, raisins, prunes, apricots, black strap molasses, 1 tsp anise, 100% grape juice. These are put together in a large pitcher, topped with the grape juice and left on the kitchen counter to soak overnight. Refrigerate. Drink 4 oz. morning and evening. The drink can last up to one week. This in turn builds the immune system without any side effects that can result from use of iron tablets.

Activated Charcoal

Have activated charcoal handy at home. Activated charcoal is carbon (charcoal) that has been heated or treated with oxygen to increase its adsorptive ability. Activated charcoal traps many types of chemicals and toxins through its many tiny pores. It is used in water filters through specialized purification processes. Its many uses include:

- Detoxifying the body
- Treating infection from bacteria
- Absorbing chemicals
- Washing chemicals
- Treating insect, spider, and snake bites
- Treating poisoning of all kinds
- Treating stomach and intestinal distress
- Reducing inflammation

General Guidelines for Multi-Cellular Living

- Treating pain
- Making poultices

Vitamin Supplements

In the context of a healthy diet and lifestyle, reduction in the use of vitamin supplements while increasing the use of whole-plant foods is suggested. This will help to avoid the incidence of negative interactions among drugs and between drugs and natural remedies.

Sleep and Exercise

Sleep, eat well, exercise. Sleeping and exercise habits affect blood sugar. Therefore, getting enough sleep and movement helps to heal the body, as the organs do require activity, rest, and rejuvenation. Cancer, weight gain, diabetes, and other health challenges are helped when you get adequate sleep. It is best to sleep in darkness. A hormone called melatonin, produced by the pineal gland in the brain, helps to regulate the relationship with light and darkness, day and night. It is produced by the body during the dark portion of the day. This becomes the precursor to sleep. Melatonin, therefore, resets the body's internal clock, thus impacting the overall performance of the system. When the melatonin is functioning at peak level, the immune system is properly modulated, cell repair is in good shape. The presence of melatonin causes that feeling of sleepiness as night draws near. Keeping late hours and jobs that require many hours of wakefulness robs the body of melatonin and such persons might resort to caffeinated beverages or drugs to fight sleep. Unfortunately, such dangerous habits and use of unwholesome substances is a play on health – living life on credit.

Bathing

Bathing is different from showering. Bathing implies immersing the body in water. Having a bathtub for this purpose is very beneficial. It is rewarding to have a regular bath because it helps an individual, whether sick or healthy, to have improved respiration and digestion, and fortifies the system against colds. Bathing soothes the nerves, relaxes the muscles, and invigorates the organs, mind, and body by quickening blood circulation.

Laws of Health

Water can be used in many simple ways to treat different sicknesses. However, it is necessary for one seeking healing remedies from water to be mindful of the quality of the food consumed. In this regard, White counsels, *"The use of water can accomplish but little, if the patient does not feel the necessity of also strictly attending to his diet."*[112]

Furthermore, she writes:

> *"Many transgress the laws of health through ignorance, and they need instruction. But the greater number knows better than they do. They need to be impressed with the importance of making their knowledge a guide of life."*

General Guidelines for Multi-Cellular Living

> *"Pure air, sunlight, abstemiousness, rest, exercise, proper diet, the use of water, trust in divine power--these are the true remedies. Every person should have a knowledge of nature's remedial agencies and how to apply them."* [113]

If these were true and applicable to the health conditions of that period in history, it is very relevant today to advance this advice to the *curators* of health care and to whom she further writes:

> *"The true physician is an educator. He recognizes his responsibility, not only to the sick who are under his direct care, but also to the community in which he lives. He stands as a guardian of both physical and moral health. It is his endeavor not only to teach right methods for the treatment of the sick, but to encourage right habits of living, and to spread knowledge of right principles."* [114]

One who does not apply spiritual laws to daily living is in danger of failing in this life and in the life to come. Likewise, a failure to apply the natural laws of living to the life sooner or later manifests in weakness in both spheres of life. The physical and spiritual must go together for an experience of abundant living. Some are 'temporarily' healed of their diseases by the providential intervention of God, either by orthodox or allopathic approach to healing, and they think everything is okay and they need not to do anything more. To this, D. L. Moody's comment on baptism of the Holy Spirit and spiritual growth is very applicable to the physical. He says:

> *"Many think that because they were filled once that they are filled forever. Oh, my friend, we are porous vessels; it is necessary for us to constantly remain under the fountain in order to be full."*[115]

God has given us the fountain of chlorophyll (from vegetables), phytonutrients (from fruits) and minerals and vitamins (from nuts, grains, and seeds), and aromatic essences (essential oils from plants) for nourishment and healing of our 'porous' bodies – subject to infiltrations and attack by chemicals, stress, and unhealthy conditions of living. Just as we need a continual baptism of the Holy Spirit to remain sane in the Lord, so also do we need a continual dose of these elements (*with faith and trust in divine power*) for physical, emotional and mental clarity. To buttress this understanding, E. G. White writes:

> *"Those who choose to be presumptuous, saying, 'The Lord has healed me, and I need not restrict my diet; I can eat and drink as I please,' will erelong need, in body and soul, the restoring power of God. Because the Lord has graciously healed you, you must not think you can link yourselves up with the self-indulgent practices of the world. Do as Christ commanded after His work of healing--"go, and sin no more." John 8:11. Appetite must not be your god."*[116]

Thus, there has to be a spiritual and physical continuum. Whatever food goes inside our body either desecrates or honors it. It is important to note that disease in animals is increasing so rapidly that subsisting on animal flesh, whether it flies, swims, or walks, is highly objectionable. It is better to avoid animal flesh than to eat

General Guidelines for Multi-Cellular Living

grains and vegetables second hand. This begs no explanation because the animal – the eater, receives the nutrition that produces their growth from these natural things, and then we receive it by eating their dead lifeless flesh. How much more beneficial would it have been to obtain that nutrition fresh from the plants provided by God!

> *"As in the natural, so in the spiritual world. The natural life is preserved moment by moment by divine power; yet it is not sustained by a direct miracle, but through the use of blessings placed within our reach. So, the spiritual life is sustained by the use of those means that Providence has supplied."*[117]

The need for health – veganism (plant-based eating) and fitness as promoted in the present-day New York Borough of Brooklyn[118] is a global movement gaining more momentum each day. Most health and fitness programs focus predominantly on just the physical aspect of wellness. It is important to know that good health means more than not being sick.

I resonate well with Dr. Sears' philosophy of health and wellness, which focuses on four pillars of health: Lifestyle, Exercise, Attitude, and Nutrition (L.E.A.N.). This book approaches health and healing from a restorative standpoint; it does not uphold the principle of *grazing* – eating small meals almost round the clock – as advocated by some, including medical practitioners. As said earlier, such an approach to eating is anti-human to the digestive anatomy. A biblical understanding of health as the harmonious functioning of physical, mental, emotional, social and spiritual faculties does not support such an approach. This understanding focuses on at least eight pillars of health. In Mark 12:30 and other references in the New Testament, it is recorded that Jesus said, "*Love the Lord your God with all your heart and with all your soul and with all your mind and with all your strength.*" Healthy living, therefore, encompasses the total man:

Heart: the emotional

Soul: the spiritual

Mind: the mental

Strength: the physical

Neighbor: the social

From Jesus's statement, one can safely infer that disease comes from a violation of four laws:

> ➤ **Violation of mental and emotional laws.** Prolonged periods of negative thinking contribute to disease. Bible statements that justify this include Proverbs 23:7; 12:23, Job 3:25. Moreover, Proverbs 15:13-17; 17:22 focus on cheerfulness, contentment, and cultivating a merry heart. Finding time for laughter is good medicine. God does not want humans to be mechanical like robots but to find time for healthy relationships and laughter. We are advised to focus our minds on pure things for healthy

minds (Philippians 4:8-9). Here is an amazing statement on how our thinking affects our health. Persons who practice the biblical health laws are bound to have mental clarity and good blood circulation; they are more certain about understanding/interpreting spiritual things and hearing the voice of the Holy Spirit, which guides and shields us in the complex issues of life.

"Sickness of the mind prevails everywhere. Nine tenths of the diseases from which men suffer have their foundation here...remorse for sin sometimes undermines the constitution and unbalances the mind."[119]

Is it any wonder that suicides, mental health clinics, and drugs abound today?

➢ **Violation of God's moral and spiritual laws.** In the beginning we read about the first human pair, Adam and Eve (Genesis 3), who developed the illness of shame, blame, guilt, fear, and jealousy in their offspring, which ultimately resulted in one killing the other. We read how Jesus, after healing a paralyzed man, told him to sin no more lest a worse thing happen to him (John 5). We read other stories of sickness, resulting from sin in the heart like the case of King David – depression (Psalm 32); Miriam – jealousy and evil speaking – leprosy (Numbers 12); and the Corinthian believers of whom the apostle

Paul reported that they were eating holy communion with unclean hearts and thus getting sick and even dying (1 Corinthians 11).

- ➢ **Violation of the social laws.** The story of the 'good Samaritan' discredits discrimination, illustrates good neighborliness, social justice application, compassion, and love (Luke 10: 25-37). The Word further says if one knows what is good, it is ethical to do it otherwise it becomes a violation of that which is right (James 4:17).
- ➢ **Violation of physical laws.** These laws govern the health of our bodies. Violation of dietary and exercise laws can result in sickness. The choice of processed food above whole plant-based foods, and scanty exercise can gradually lead to illness.

Revealing God's Glory

Sometimes sickness might be a way by which God seeks to make man glorify His name; sickness can be a means of making one realize the goodness of God and the value of turning to Him as the only possessor of healing power. The Bible tells the story of persons like King David, who said he was afflicted because of his sin in Psalm 119: 67, 71:

> "Before I was afflicted, I went astray, but now I keep Your word...It is good for me that I have been afflicted, that I may learn Your statutes."

So, we infer that God may permit sickness so that the individual can correct his ways and turn to Him. In the case of Lazarus in John 11:1-4, Jesus said the sickness was for the purpose of glorifying God. His family, friends, and followers glorified God for giving him life again, and so they learned the power and the hope in resurrection from this incident. In John 9:3, when Jesus was asked about the man who was blind from birth,

> *"Jesus answered, 'Neither this man nor his parents sinned, but that the works of God should be revealed in him."*

But Christ healed him. Job's story is a classic example of God showcasing His power to heal even in the face of serious torment and health harassment by Satan. Ultimately, God came through for Job by showing His glory, healing and restoring him beyond his former state. Moreover, the apostle Paul, in 2 Corinthians 12:7-12, had repeatedly pleaded with God to remove "a thorn in his flesh," but God said to him, *"My grace is sufficient for you, for my strength is made perfect in weakness."* From the conversation, it appears that Paul had a disposition to be proud and boastful and so God made a way to protect him from the sin of pride.

We learn, therefore, that God permits certain illnesses to show His glory, while in some other cases (Paul and David), He uses sickness to get our attention so we may remain close to Him.

Sometimes, the genuineness or faithfulness in one's faith might not guarantee deliverance or total physical healing. Jesus - the great physician (Matthew 9:12) and mighty healer, reserves the prerogative to choose to heal or not. Even when He does not, His grace is always sufficient and sustaining spiritually and emotionally. He can use the physically broken human vessel to be a witness to others in this life, who are looking forward to a new world - "a new heaven and a new earth" (Revelation 21:1-4; Isaiah 67:17). There the saved will not experience any more pain or sickness.

We learn too, that diseases don't just happen. More often than not, we 'eat or live' them into our system. When this is the case, what the individual needs is a turnaround in lifestyle, to turn off the faucet from where the body gets flooded with toxins. At other times, disease is inherited from parents. When this is the case, the individual needs to carefully examine the parents' ways of living to see if there is something that could be done differently to avoid or reduce the weight or effect of whatever ailed them that got transmitted to their offspring. Sometimes disease is acquired from the living environment. This calls for great carefulness in what exposures trap the individual. It is important to God, as one who balances justice and mercy in

General Guidelines for Multi-Cellular Living

all things. He is the ultimate healer, and values obedience. Here is a startling quotation in this regard. White writes:

> "Many have expected that God would keep them from sickness merely because they have asked Him to do so. But God did not regard their prayers, because their faith was not made perfect by works. God will not work a miracle to keep those from sickness who have no care for themselves, but are continually violating the laws of health, and make no efforts to prevent disease. When we do all we can on our part to have health, then may we expect that the blessed results will follow, and we can ask God in faith to bless our efforts for the preservation of health. He will then answer our prayer, if His name can be glorified thereby. But let all understand that they have a work to do. God will not work in a miraculous manner to preserve the health of persons who are taking a sure course to make themselves sick, by their careless inattention to the laws of health. ... Many, as their last resort, follow the directions in the word of God, and request the prayers of the elders of the church for their restoration to health. God does not see fit to answer prayers offered in behalf of such, for He knows that if they should be restored to health, they would again sacrifice it upon the altar of unhealthy appetite."[120]

Obedience is not a very common virtue today, but good health is the reward of obedience to God.

It is important to emphasize the benefits of gardening to the entire family, not just for the provision of food but for strength of the body, development of the mind, and building of character. God wants the hands to be directly in touch with nature – plants. When Adam and Eve were made, God put them in a garden so they could have activity, which is essential for happiness (Genesis 2:15). This earth is a practice ground for the world to come. As much as is possible, families and individuals should find time and space to garden. For those who have children, gardening provides the time and space for them to learn the things of nature. They will learn that God tenderly cultivates the soil of the soul – the mind, as humans cultivate plants, flowers, and crops. In the earth made new, the redeemed will engage in building and planting (Isaiah 65:21, 22).

To the Physician

As written by Ellen G. White,

> "The only hope of better things is in the education of the people in right principles. Let physicians teach the people that restorative power is not in drugs, but in nature."[121]

It is estimated that medications could be the third most common cause of death after heart disease and cancer. Whereas disease is an effort of nature to free the system from conditions that result from a violation of the laws of health, the principle is not common knowledge. It therefore is the responsibility of medical educators to respect and propagate this knowledge. Thus, says inspired writing,

> "In case of sickness, the cause should be ascertained. Unhealthful conditions should be changed, wrong habits corrected, then nature is to be assisted in her effort to expel impurities and re-establish right conditions in the system. In order to save more lives, it is the duty of Godly physicians to prescribe a change of heart in place of drugs."[122]

This is a u-turn to plant-based eating. Such a change transplants in the mind, a choice, to determine or not to cooperate with the heavenly designer of the human frame -

General Guidelines for Multi-Cellular Living

to make those inner changes that would transform inside out. It is, therefore, still possible for an honest doctor to practice honest medicine. Physicians should encourage families along the lines of preventive or lifestyle medicine. In this direction, the words of Dr. Christiaan Barnard who conducted the first ever heart transplant rings a bell. He said,

> *"I have saved the lives of 150 people with heart transplantations. If I had focused on preventive medicine earlier, I would have saved 150 million."*

If when we become ill, we understood that we have brought this illness upon ourselves and seek out the ways in which we have been disobedient to God's laws and correct our living habits and re-establish right conditions by our understanding and right actions, we would get well without taking medication or drugs of any sort. It is vital that we cease to treat disease as an enemy. We must understand that "Disease" is the cure, the effort of nature to cleanse itself. This cannot be too often repeated for it is not understood in any way but by few current (contemporary) doctors. Some physicians, like Dr. Aseem Malhotra, in the video titled *Profit Over Population Health at the European Parliament*, are recognizing that lifestyle change is more powerful than any drug, and such a change has no side effects. You can watch the video at the following location:

https://www.youtube.com/watch?v=jcnd3usdNxo&t=5s

Naturally we get sick and do not know the cause. In fear we turn to the doctors who use drug prescriptions and receive our drug treatments. They, for the most part, have been educated to depend on the use of pharmaceuticals. In the article, "Disease – Friend or Enemy," Dr. J. Terrel [123]explains the disease process and how it can be a friend to warn about the deficiencies of the body before it becomes too late. Physicians must not reject the authority of Christ in their healing methods but must recognize that *"Physical healing is a science of heavenly birth, bound up with the gospel commission."*[124] As time permits, physicians will do well to incorporate integrative health methods into their practices for optimal results in **well-care** as opposed to **sick-care.**

We learn, in the final analysis, that God will heal. Natural healing using the laws of health is available to all humans regardless of religious affiliation or location. It is not His desire that we suffer, but that we stay in health. God cares about how we feel; He cares about our bodies, and daily He educates us that disease should practically remind us that the wages of sin (disobedience to physical or moral laws) is death. Many places in scripture offer quotations that support the notion that God is interested in blessing even our food and water and will take sickness away so that we may live. (For example, see Exodus 23:25). God's blessings are simple solutions conditioned on obedience to the natural

General Guidelines for Multi-Cellular Living

and moral laws He has instituted for our physical, moral and spiritual sustenance. His healing always falls in harmony with natural laws. God cares about life and even animals were born to live and not to be brutally murdered and consumed. Addition of 'dead matter' from the animal kingdom to human nutrition has continued to negatively impact the delicate and wonderful human infrastructure.

The Bible is replete with stories to illustrate and justify the relationship between the physical state of man and the spiritual. In summation, the best approach to balanced living is ultimately complete in the application of GOD's PLAN – obedience.

"Come, all you who are thirsty,
come to the waters;
and you who have no money,
come, buy and eat!
Come, buy wine and milk
without money and without cost.
Why spend money on what is not bread,
and your labor on what does not satisfy?
Listen, listen to me, and eat what is good,
and you will delight in the richest of fare...
Let the wicked forsake their ways and the unrighteous their thoughts. Let them turn to the LORD, and he will have mercy on them, and to our God, for he will freely pardon."

Simple Solutions

Isaiah 55: 1, 2, 7; Isaiah 61:1-3

God in His providence has given man natural foods for sustenance so that he can make intelligent choices. He desires human happiness, so He says in John 13:17, that we shall be happy if we 'know' and do 'these things', which includes being careful about the internal care of our body temple. If God could restore proud King Nebuchadnezzar (Daniel 4:34), He can restore anyone else. Daniel and his friends set the pace. Everything one needs to know about nutrition is summarized in GOD'S PLAN. In a world filled with physical, emotional, and spiritual bruises from sin, it is God's plan to restore man to his original image – a state of perfect health. True and believing children of God are those who hold onto and practice the moral and health laws (*truths- and the Bible calls such persons "righteous"*), all of which come from the same source - God. Such persons will experience restoration here in this mortal life, and they are promised ultimate restoration at the resurrection and recreation of the righteous (1 Corinthians 15:51-53), an event which will take place at the end of time – the second coming of Jesus Christ, the Son of God. However, the power of science in this age, the greatest of all sciences is yet to be seriously noised about. That is the science of salvation, which is an opportunity available within the reach of all persons today.

General Guidelines for Multi-Cellular Living

A Taste of Heaven by Dr. Ekele Nwankwo is a video introduction of simple food creations at a home setting. You can watch this introductory video at the following location:

https://www.youtube.com/watch?v=Kl7dkxSsHpA
More detailed videos on making local soups, and cheese and egg substitutes are available on the You Tube Channel.

Home-made plant-based dishes

Veggie burger crumbles re-steamed with onions and a little oil.

Vegetable soups: okora, and egusi; served with pounded yam, fufu, garri, or whole wheat/oat flour.

The conclusion of the whole matter is:

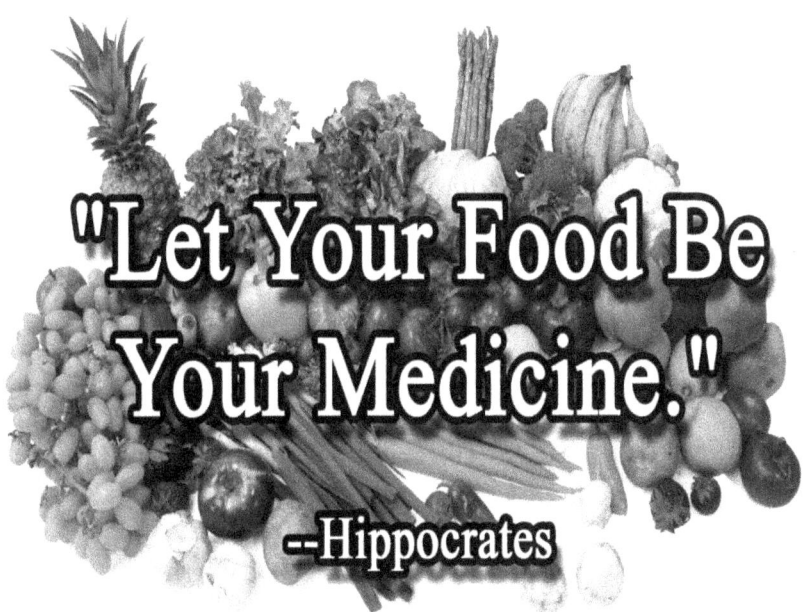

"And the very God of peace sanctify you wholly; and I pray God your whole spirit and soul and body be preserved blameless unto the coming of our Lord Jesus Christ."
1 Thessalonians 5:23 (KJV)

Simple Solutions

Author's Biographical Sketch

Ekele Ukegbu-Nwankwo is a devoted Christian board-certified chaplain and natural health consultant. Using her skills, she fosters a holistic transformational system for individuals who desire sustainable change. Her counseling includes information on disease prevention and reversal, and the link between nutrition and mental health. She organizes and conducts plant-based cooking classes, and coaches in aromatherapy and crafting of essential oil blends.

Dr. Ekele has worked as a health-care chaplain since 2006, and a lifestyle consultant since 2010. As a seasoned chaplain, she provides a passionate combination of pastoral care and health counseling. These specialized skills help her clients make informed choices on wellness and the attainment of their personal life goals.

Ekele holds a Doctor of Ministry (D. Min) degree in health care chaplaincy from Andrews University; a Doctor of Naturopathy degree in Original Medicine (DNOM) from the International Institute of Original Medicine (IIOM), and a post graduate diploma in Education (PGDE). She is a certified *Dr. Sears Wellness* coach.

Born and raised in Nigeria, Ekele currently resides in Ohio, USA, and has four adult children.

Contact Information

Connect with me on my website: www.liv-n-glow.com

Connect with me by email: info@liv-n-glow.com

Appendix

Some Tropical Fruits and Vegetables of Nigeria and West Africa

Avocado pear

Banana

Mangos

Guava

Simple Solutions

Watermelon

Pawpaw (Papaya)

Oranges and Tangerines

Cucumber

Some Tropical Fruits and Vegetables of Nigeria and West Africa

Pineapple

Cashews

Star Apples

Lemons

Simple Solutions

Green apples from Jos

Velvet tamarind (nkwa)

Soursop (graviola)

Coconut

Some Tropical Fruits and Vegetables of Nigeria and West Africa

Tropical almonds

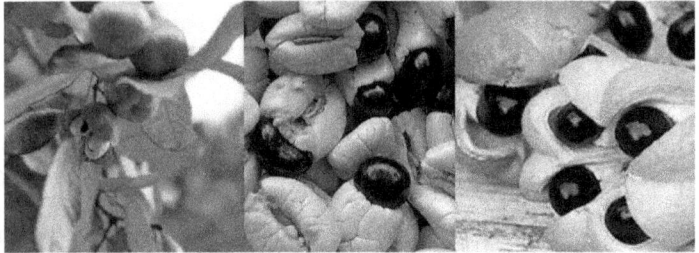

Ackee (much more found in West Indian islands)

Fluted pumpkin (ugu)

Water leaf

Simple Solutions

Garden egg leaf and fruit (opkokwa)

Bitter leaf

African spinach (green)

Date fruits

Some Tropical Fruits and Vegetables of Nigeria and West Africa

African walnuts (ukpa)

Pepper fruit (nmimi)

Tomatoes

Celery

Simple Solutions

Pitanga berries (cherry)

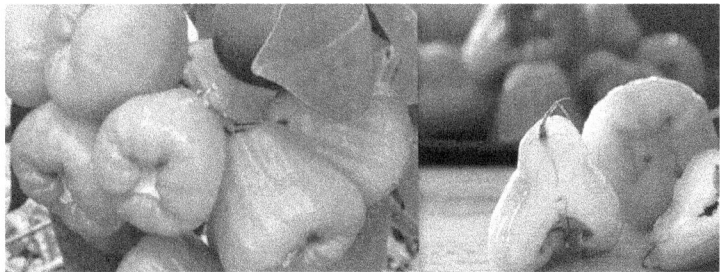
Rose or water apples

Hog plums

Grapefruit

Some Tropical Fruits and Vegetables of Nigeria and West Africa

Tangerines

Lime

Carrots

African bush pears (ube & yellow corn)

Tropical garden eggs (anara fruits)

Asparagus

Yellow monkey kola (ochicha)

Some Tropical Fruits and Vegetables of Nigeria and West Africa

Nigerian local strawberry (Jos area)

https://www.finelib.com/about/tropical-fruits-and-vegetables/19

There are other fruits, root crops, and vegetables commercially produced like the cola nut, oil palm fruits, bush mango or ugiri (produces ogbono), sorghum, cowpeas, yams, plantains and okora. Many of these are seasonal while some are nearly becoming extinct. The economy and health of its citizens would be greatly benefited if the government could pay attention to mechanizing the farming, preservation, and promotion of the consumption of these nutritious indigenous foods.

Simple Solutions

Notes

[1] Ellen G. White, *Desire of ages*, (Mountain View, CA: Pacific Press Publishing Assoc., 1898, 1940), 824.

[2] Maxwell C. Ukegbu, *Basic biblical truths and Satan's attempt to distort and/or change them*, PortHarcourt, Nigeria: Neokecci Multiconcepts, 2008), 86-87.

[3] *United Church of God: Beyond today*, https://www.ucg.org/bible-study-tools/booklets/what-does-the-bible-teach-about-clean-and-unclean-meats/infographic-which

[4] Ellen G. White, *Counsels on diet and foods*, (Hagerstown, MD: Review and Herald Publishing Association, 1905, 1938 – 2001 edition), 384-385.

[5] *Journal of Infectious Disease and Preventive Medicine*, https://www.omicsonline.org/open-access/pharaohs-and-mummies-diseases-of-ancient-egypt-and-modern-approaches-2329-8731.1000e110.php?aid=20477&view=mobile (October 12, 2013)

[6] Ibid.

[7] https://www.llu.edu/assets/news/today/documents/today102705.pdf

[8] https://www.youtube.com/watch?v=j_xpACSjggc

[9] https://www.youtube.com/watch?v=Onhtdxf8-No

[10] Ellen G. White, *Counsels on diet and foods*, (Hagerstown, MD: Review and Herald Publishing Association, 1905, 1938 – 2001 edition), 373.

[11] Ellen G. White, *Spiritual gifts*, Vol. 4, part 1, (1864), 154-156.

[12] http://www.biblestudy.org/maps/life-span-of-bible-patriarchs-before-after-the-flood.html

[13] Ellen G. White, *Ministry of healing*, (Nampa, ID: Pacific Press Publishing, 1909), page 127.

[14] Ellen G. White, *Counsels on health*, (Mountain View, CA: Pacific Press Publishing Association, 1951), 37.

[15] Denise Winterman, *Breakfast, lunch, dinner: Have we always eaten them?* https://www.bbc.com/news/magazine-20243692 (November 15, 2012).

[16] David Paulson, *Signs of the times* (Harvest Ingathering, 1915).

17 *How to Live*, http://www.present-truth.org/7-Health-Secrets-Sem/SOP/HOW%20TO%20LIVE.pdf

18 Ellen G. White, *Patriarchs and prophets*, (Hagerstown, MD: Review and Herald Publishing Association, 1868), 443.

19 Ellen G. White, *Counsels on diet and foods*, (Hagerstown, MD: Review and Herald Publishing Association, 1905, 1938 – 2001 edition), 277.

20 Ibid., 21.2

21 Ellen G. White, (Letter 208, 1906).

22 *Seventh-day Adventists believe*, (Mountain View, CA: Pacific Press Publishing Association, 2015), 278.

23 "Vegetarians have reduced risks of certain diseases because of their increased consumption of whole grains, dried beans, nuts, fresh and dried fruits, and vegetables. Vegetarians are exposed to fewer carcinogens and mutagens because they do not eat meat." http://www.adventistreport.com/2012/12/the-seventh-day-adventist-position.html#sthash.nbvxbTx7.dpuf

24 Elissa Kido, "For real education reform, take a cue from the Adventists," *Christian Science Monitor*, Weekly Digital Edition, (November 15, 2010).

25 Ellen G. White, *Ministry of healing*, (Nampa, ID: Pacific Press Publishing, 1909), 127. "Pure air, sunlight, abstemiousness, rest, exercise, proper diet, the use of water, trust in divine power—these are the true remedies."

26 Neil Nedley, *Proof positive: Milk* (Ardmore, OK: Quality Books Inc, 1999), 151.

27 Ibid., 150.

28 C. M. Weaver, "Calcium bioavailability and its relation to osteoporosis," *Proceedings of the Society for Experimental Biology and Medicine*, (June 1992, 200(2)). Quoted from Nedley, 155: "Although milk has a high calcium content, 60 to 80 percent of it is not absorbed through the human intestine"

29 Don Colbert, *Toxic Relief* (Lake Mary, FL: Siloam, 2003), 31.

30 T. Colin Campbell and Thomas M. Campbell, *The China study: The most comprehensive study of nutrition ever conducted and the startling implications of diet, weight-loss and long-term health*, (Dallas, TX: BenBella, 2006), 205.

31 Ellen G. White, *Counsels on diet and foods*, (Hagerstown, MD: Review and Herald Publishing Association, 1905, 1938 – 2001 edition), 386.

Notes

[32] Ellen G. White, *Testimonies for the Church*, Vol. 1, (Ellen G. White Publications, 1855, copyright, 1948), 466.

[33] Ellen G. White, Article A, (Hagerstown, MD: Review and Herald, May 27, 1902).

[34] *Soy Info Center*, 2004 (Unpublished Manuscript), http://www.soyinfocenter.com/HSS/harry_miller.php

[35] Connie Weaver, "Should dairy be recommended as part of a healthy vegetarian diet?" *American Journal of Clinical Nutrition* 89 (2009):2 -3.

[36] Neil Nedley, *Proof positive: Milk*, (Ardmore, OK: Quality Books Inc, 1999), 249.

[37] T. Colin Campbell and Thomas M. Campbell, *The China study: The most comprehensive study of nutrition ever conducted and the startling implications of diet, weight-loss and long-term health*, (Dallas, TX: BenBella, 2006), 276.

[38] M. Greger, *How much pus is there in milk?* (2011), https://nutritionfacts.org/2011/09/08/how-much-pus-is-there-in-milk/

[39] "Reducing the environmental impact of dietary choice: Perspectives from a behavioral and social change approach," *Journal of Environmental and Public Health* 2 (2012). Article ID 978672, doi: 10.1155/2012/978672.

[40] Ellen G. White, *Counsels on diet and foods*, (Hagerstown, MD: Review and Herald Publishing Association, 1905, 1938 – 2001 edition), 365.

[41] Ibid., 322 (Letter 70, 1896).

[42] Ibid., 384, 385, 386.

[43] Vance Farrell, *International meat crisis: The meat you eat is contaminated and infected to a degree never before known in human history*, (Altamonte, TN: Harvestime Books, 2001), 6, 23, 24.

[44] Barbara Stitt, *Food and behavior: a natural connection*, (Manitowoc, WI: Natural Press, 1997), 37.

[45] Ellen G. White, *Counsels on diet and foods*, (Hagerstown, MD: Review and Herald Publishing Association, 1905, 1938 – 2001 edition), 179.

[46] *Meal frequency and timing in health and disease*, (2014). https://www.ncbi.nlm.nih.gov/pmc/articles/PMC4250148/

[47] Ellen G. White, Manuscript 3, 1897.

[48] Arnold Ehrets, *Rational fasting: For physical, mental and spiritual rejuvenation*, (Summertown, TN: Ehret Literature Publishing Company, 2013), 22.

[49] Ellen G. White, *Ministry of healing* (Nampa, ID: Pacific Press Publishing, 1909), 127.

[50] Arnold Ehrets, *Rational fasting: For physical, mental and spiritual rejuvenation*, (Summertown, TN: Ehret Literature Publishing Company, 2013), 98.

[51] P. J. Benjamin and F. M. Tappan, *Tappan's Hand Book of Healing Massage Techniques*, (Upper Saddle River, NJ: Pearson Education, Inc., 2005), 9.

[52] L. Cordain, S. Eaton, and A. Sebastian, "Origins and evolution of the western diet: Health implications for the 21st century 1, 2," *American Journal of Clinical Nutrition,* 81(2) (2005): 341-354.

[53] Ellen G. White, *Counsels on diet and foods*, (Hagerstown, MD: Review and Herald Publishing Association, 1905, 1938 – 2001 edition), 272.

[54] Pedro Carrera-Bastos, Maelan Fontes-Vellalba, James H. O'Keefe, Staffan Lindeberg, Loren Cordain, *Western diet and lifestyle and diseases of civilization*, (Hammersmith, London: Dove Press, 2011), 17.

[55] Ibid., 15.

[56] Ibid., 27.

[57] Sophie Johnson, *Intelligient squad*, (U.S. 2013 Debates, December 6, 2013), 2.

[58] Annia Ciedzadlo, "Does the Mediterranean diet even exist"? *International New York Times*, April 1, 2011, 1.

[59] Olayiwola et al., "Demographic characteristics and dietary pattern of the elderly in Ondo State, Nigeria," *BJM & MR* 3(4), (2013): 2178. Science Domain International, www.sciencedomain.org

[60] *The State of US Health, 1990 to 2016*, April 10, 2018, https://jamanetwork.com/journals/jama/fullarticle/2678018

[61] Ellen G. White, *Counsels on diet and foods*, (Hagerstown, MD: Review and Herald Publishing Association, 1903, 1938 – 2001 edition),.400.

[62] Ellen G. White, *Ministry of healing,* (Nampa, ID: Pacific Press Publishing, 1909).

[63] *Country life natural foods nutritional seminar cookbook*, (Teach Services, Inc., 1996), 42.

Notes

[64] *SDA encyclopedia*, (1976), 574, 5. B

[65] T. Colin Campbell and Thomas M. Campbell, *The China study: The most comprehensive study of nutrition ever conducted and the startling implications of diet, weight-loss and long-term health*, (Dallas, TX: BenBella, 2006), 76.

[66] Ibid., 205.

[67] Don Colbert, *Toxic relief*, (Lake Mary, FL: Siloam, 2003), 31.

[68] Isaac Akinyele, *Ensuring food and nutrition security in rural Nigeria: an assessment of the challenges, information needs, and analytical capacity*, (Abuja: International Food Policy Research Institute (IFPRI), Nigeria Strategy Support Program (NSSP 007), 2009), 4. "Food security refers to the condition in which all people, at all times, have physical, social, and economic access to sufficient, safe, and nutritious food that meets their dietary needs and food preferences for an active and healthy life (FAO/WHO 1992; FAO 1996). Food availability, stability of supplies and food access are related determinants of food security."
http://www.ifpri.org/sites/default/files/publications/nsspbp07.pdf

[69] People for the Ethical Treatment of Animals (PeTA), *The chicken industry*, "Virtually all chickens raised for their flesh (or "broiler chickens" as they are referred to by the meat industry), spend their lives crammed into massive, windowless sheds that typically hold as many as 40,000 birds each."
http://www.peta.org/issues/animals-used-for-food/factory-farming/chickens/chicken-industry/#ixzz2xtr124jh

[70] Ellen G. White, *Counsels on diet and foods*, (Hagerstown, MD: Review and Herald Publishing Association, 1905, 1938 – 2001 edition), 385-386.

[71] Ibid., 262.

[72] J. O. Omokhodion, "Linking the dominance of house girls in Nigeria households to the girl-child socialization pattern in Nigeria." *Current Research Journal of Social Sciences* 1(2) (Maxwell Scientific Organization, 2009), 2041-3246.

[73] Ellen G. White, *Testimonies for the church*, Vol. 2, (Ellen G. White Publications, 1855, copyright, 1948), 370.

74 T. Colin Campbell and Thomas M. Campbell, *The China study: The most comprehensive study of nutrition ever conducted and the startling implications of diet, weight-loss and long-term health*, (Dallas, TX: BenBella, 2006), 66.

75 Mike Anderson, *Rave diet and lifestyle: The natural foods diet with meals that heal*, (RaveDiet, 2009), 104,105.

76 Matt Price, *What is hemp? Understanding the differences between hemp and cannabis*, https://www.medicaljane.com/2015/01/14/the-differences-between-hemp-and-cannabis/

77 https://www.projectcbd.org/guidance/conditions

78 Steven Gundry, *Plant paradox: The hidden dangers in "healthy" foods that cause disease and weight gain*. (New York, NY: Harper Wave; April 25, 2017).

79 https://www.muscleforlife.com/plant-paradox/.

80 Ellen G. White, *Counsels on diet and foods*, (Hagerstown, MD: Review and Herald Publishing Association, 1905, 1938 – 2001 edition), 81.

81 "Fat, sick, and nearly dead," (Directed by Joe Cross, Kurt Engfehr, 2010).

82 "Forks over knives," (Made by Lee Fulkerson, 2011).

83 Ellen G. White, *Counsels on diet and foods*, (Hagerstown, MD: Review and Herald Publishing Association, 1905, 1938 – 2001 edition), 173.

84 Ellen G. White, *Spiritual gifts*, Vol. 4a, (1864), 133.

85 Ibid, 272.

86 Ellen G. White, *Ministry of healing*, (Nampa, ID: Pacific Press Publishing, 1909), 302, 303.

87 Jim Sharps, *Original Health Secrets.com*, 2014.

88 Ellen G. White, *The dress reform*, PH134 11.1 & 2.

89 Ellen G. White, *Testimonies for the church*, Vol. 2, (Ellen G. White Publications, 1855, copyright, 1948), 643.

90 M. Wilson, D. Wilson, *God's medical kit*. (Savannah, TN: Centurion Ministry, 2010)

91 David Stewart, *Healing oils of the Bible*, (Marble Hill, MO: Care Publications, 2003), 37.

92 Ellen G. White, *Christ's object lessons*, (Hagerstown, MD: Review and Herald, 2002).

93 Ellen G. White, *Testimonies for the church*, Vol. 6, (Ellen G. White Publications, 1855, copyright, 1948), 350.

Notes

[94] Marian O. Atolagbe, *Nature's tasty meals and remedies*, (Ogun State: Iperu-Remo, 2014), 24.

[95] Ibid., 15.

[96] Jim Sharps, (2011). *Basic principles of total health: Harmonious integration of body, mind, and spirit.* 8, 13.

[97] Ellen G. White, *Counsels on diet and foods*, (Hagerstown, MD: Review and Herald Publishing Association, 1905, 1938 – 2001 edition), 345.

[98] Jo Ann Davidson, "An Atheist Confirms Ellen White's Counsel," *Adventist World*, 3/1/2019.

[99] David Stewart, Chemistry of Essential Oils Made Simple: God's Love Manifest in Molecules, 1st edition, (Marble Hill, MO: Care Publications, 2005), 447, 448, 490.

[100] David Stewart, *Healing oils of the Bible*, 1st edition, (Marble Hill, MO: Care Publications, 2002), 27, 29.

[101] T. Colin Campbell and Thomas M. Campbell, *The China study: The most comprehensive study of nutrition ever conducted and the startling implications of diet, weight-loss and long-term health*, (Dallas, TX: BenBella, 2006), 17.

[102] Ty M. Bolinger, *Cancer step outside the box*, 6th edition, EBook, (Infinity 510^2 Partners, 2014), 352, 353.

[103] James Howenstine, *Physician's guide to natural health products that work*, Miami, FL: Penhurst books, 2007).

[104] Ellen G. White, *Counsels on diet and foods*, (Hagerstown, MD: Review and Herald Publishing Association, 1905, 1938 – 2001 edition), 327.

[105] Ibid., 345.

[106] J. Terrell, Article: http://www.ellenwhitedefend.com/SOP-Library/Health/Disease-Friend-enemy.pdf

[107] Neal Barnard, Physicians' Committee for Responsible Medicine.

[108] Ann Marie Helmenstine, *How much of your body is water?* (Online article, April 30, 2018), https://www.thoughtco.com/how-much-of-your-body-is-water-609406

[109] *Fiber content of food – Prebiotin, Prebiotic (NIH).* (Online article), https://www.prebiotin.com/prebiotin-academy/fiber-content-of-foods/

110 The Daily Mail, *Could you eat all your meals before 3pm?* (May 2018), https://www.dailymail.co.uk/health/article-5715613/Study-finds-eat-meals-3pm.html

111 Ellen G. White, *Counsels on diet and foods*, (Hagerstown, MD: Review and Herald Publishing Association, 1905, 1938 – 2001 edition), 16, 18.

112 Ibid., 304.4.

113 Ellen G. White, *Ministry of healing* (Nampa, ID: Pacific Press Publishing, 1909), 125 – 127.

114 Ibid.

115 D. L. Moody, *They found the secret*, 85, 86; quoted in "Steps to Personal Revival…" by Helmut Haubeil, 53.

116 Ellen G. White, *Counsels on diet and foods*, (Hagerstown, MD: Review and Herald Publishing Association, 1905, 1938 – 2001 edition), 25.

117 Ellen G. White, *Acts of the Apostles*, (Mountain View, CA: Pacific Press Publishing Association, 1911), 284.2.

118 "Vegan Brooklyn Borough President Eric Adams Launches Plant." (New York Times, January 2, 2017) https://www.nytimes.com

119 Ellen G. White, *Mind, Character and Personality*, (Hagerstown, MD: Review and Herald Publishing Association, 1999), 59.

120 Ellen G. White, *Counsels on diet and foods*, (Hagerstown, MD: Review and Herald Publishing Association, 1905, 1938 – 2001 edition), 26.

121 Ellen G. White, *Counsels on Health*, (Mountain View, CA: Pacific Press Publishing Association), 90.1.

122 Ibid.

123 J. Terrell, Article: http://www.ellenwhitedefend.com/SOP-Library/Health/Disease-Friend-enemy.pdf

124 Ellen G. White, *Medical Ministry,* (Mountain View, CA: Pacific Press Publishing Association), 320.

www.ingramcontent.com/pod-product-compliance
Lightning Source LLC
Chambersburg PA
CBHW050442240426
43661CB00055B/2474